...VICE CENTER
Service Programs
1368 LINCOLN AVENUE, SUITE 108
SAN RAFAEL, CA 94901
(415) 459-2234

CAMBRIDGE STUDIES IN CRIMINOLOGY XLII

General Editor: Sir Leon Radzinowicz

COMMUNITY SERVICE ORDERS

THE HEINEMANN LIBRARY OF CRIMINOLOGY
AND PENAL REFORM

CAMBRIDGE STUDIES IN CRIMINOLOGY

COMMUNITY SERVICE ORDERS

The development and use of
a new penal measure

by

Warren Young

HEINEMANN

LONDON

Heinemann Educational Books Ltd
22 Bedford Square, London WC1B 3HH

LONDON EDINBURGH MELBOURNE AUCKLAND
HONG KONG SINGAPORE KUALA LUMPUR NEW DELHI
IBADAN NAIROBI JOHANNESBURG
EXETER (NH) KINGSTON PORT OF SPAIN

ISBN 0 435 82975 0

Publisher's note: This series is continuous with the
Cambridge Studies in Criminology, Volumes I to XIX,
published by Macmillan & Co., London

British Library Cataloguing in Publication Data

Young, Warren
  Community Service Orders. – (Cambridge studies
  in criminology; no.42).
  1. Community-based corrections – England –
  Case studies
  I. Title II. Series
  364.6   HV9346.A5

  ISBN 0-435-82975-0

Typeset by Red Lion Setters, Holborn, London

Printed in Great Britain by
the Fakenham Press, Fakenham, Norfolk

Contents

Preface

This book is a revised version of a dissertation presented to the University of Cambridge for a Ph.D. degree. I am extremely grateful to Miss Joan King of the Institute of Criminology, Cambridge, for the invaluable advice and assistance she gave to me throughout the field research, and especially for her endless enthusiasm and inspiration. I am also grateful to Dr David Farrington for aid in statistical and computing problems, and to many others at the Institute of Criminology, Cambridge, for advice and encouragement in many different ways.

Thanks must also go to the Home Office, and to chief probation officers, chief constables, and clerks to the justices of the areas and courts upon which the research concentrated. The study would not have been possible without the extensive access I was allowed to official records. Above all, I must thank the community service organizers and their staff in Bedfordshire, Cambridgeshire, Kent, Nottinghamshire, and Suffolk for their eagerness to participate in the study, for the time that they spared to talk to me on many occasions, and for their help in allowing me unlimited access to the files and records in their offices. Their willingness to allow their schemes to be scrutinized and criticized is a reflection of their enthusiasm for the community service order and their hope that it would realize its full potential.

Finally, I am grateful to Miss Bernice Rowse for typing assistance and to my wife Robyn for her patience and endurance.

WARREN YOUNG
January 1979

vii

Introduction

The community service order is a new penal measure which was introduced under the Criminal Justice Act 1972 for any offender aged 17 and over convicted of any offence (other than murder) punishable by imprisonment. It stemmed directly from a recommendation of a sub-committee of the Home Secretary's Advisory Council on the Penal System (Home Office, 1970a), commonly known as the Wootton Committee, which was set up to consider what improvements or additions could be made to the existing range of non-custodial and semi-custodial penal measures. The recommendation was supported in a modified form by a Home Office Working Group set up to examine its feasibility.

The community service order empowers courts to sentence offenders to a period of work in the community, of not less than forty hours but no more than 240, under the supervision of a community service organizer appointed by, and subject to the control of, the local Probation and After-care Committee. There is no legal requirement that the organizer be a qualified probation officer, but organizers throughout the country have usually been appointed from within the ranks of the probation service.

In accordance with the caveat expressed by the Wootton Committee against over-hasty implementation of an unproven measure in an uncharted field, six probation areas encompassing a wide variety of local conditions were chosen to set up pilot schemes in 1973 for an initial period of two years. The six areas were Inner London, Kent, Nottinghamshire, Durham, south-west Lancashire, and Shropshire. The initial period was designed to allow research into the practicability of the scheme and the way in which it could best be implemented.

This task fell to the Home Office Research Unit, who monitored the scheme and assessed its workability during this two-year period.[1] The research team concentrated upon an evaluation of operational features of the scheme, and thus gave little consideration to the relationship of the sentence to broader issues of penal policy. Their main concern was to establish the long-term viability of the sentence.

The pilot schemes were not without their teething troubles. The Inner London scheme, for example, reported unforeseen difficulties in the early stages, particularly with under-staffing, promises of work not materializing, and unmotivated offenders (Inner London Probation and After-care Service, 1975: pp. 3–4). Nevertheless, their development in all six areas was rapid enough to ensure that success, in terms of the continuance of the scheme, was assured. Some of the pilot areas published their own reports, expressing their undiluted support for the sentence. The more cautious declaration by the Home Office Research Unit that the measure had proved itself viable (Pease *et al.*, 1975: p. 70) was enough to persuade the Government that it was an innovation worth pursuing. The Minister of State for Home Affairs announced on 22 August 1974 (Home Office Circular no. 158/1974) that the decision had been taken to extend the opportunity to develop community service schemes to all probation and after-care areas in England and Wales from 1 April 1975.

However, a court cannot make a community service order until it 'has been notified by the Secretary of State that arrangements exist for persons who reside in the petty sessions area in which the offender resides or will reside to perform work under such orders' (Powers of Criminal Courts Act 1973 s. 14(2)). Proposals for community service schemes therefore had to be submitted for approval to the Home Office, which suggested that they be phased in gradually in each area. This advice was heeded. By 31 March 1976 the scheme was available to every court in only fifteen out of fifty-six probation and after-care areas, and by the end of 1976 the counties of Dyfed and Cornwall were still without a community service scheme in any of their petty sessional areas. Financial restrictions contributed to the delay in extending the scheme, but the initial decision for gradual development was no doubt taken with a view to ensuring that schemes were not hastily introduced without adequate planning or resources.

Despite this caution, it is clear that the community service order is now an established and important penal innovation. Indeed, it is probably the most important penal measure introduced for adults since the probation order received legislative approval in 1907. It has received the enthusiastic support of sentencers, penal administrators, and probation officers alike, and has expanded rapidly to a level undoubtedly far beyond that originally envisaged by the Wootton Committee. The number of orders passed throughout England and Wales during 1977 was 11,768—at a time when the sentence was not yet even available to all courts. Once the expansion of the scheme is complete, its use may possibly even rival that of the probation order. Indeed, there are already indications of this in some of the pilot areas where the sentence has been available for several years.

The sentence, too, is important not only because of its expansion in England, but also because of the interest and the parallel innovations which it has prompted in other countries. Apart from Tasmania—which also introduced a scheme in 1972 (called the Saturday Work Order scheme)—England was the first country to use community service work as a penal measure in itself. Since then, however, similar legislation has been introduced in British Columbia, Ontario and other provinces in Canada, several states in the United States and Australia, and New Zealand. Community service is also used in some parts of the United States as a form of non-statutory pre-trial or pre-sentence diversion. Although of course each country has its own unique problems, the lessons which can be learnt from the English experience and the form which its development has taken are relevant to overseas experiments.

This book surveys the origins and development of the community service order in England, and the way in which it is used by the courts. No other study has as yet systematically examined variations between areas in the use to which the sentence is being put and the way in which it is being implemented. This research investigates such variations, the form which they take, and the reasons why they exist. It will be shown that the development of the sentence, although evident in terms of numbers, is still unclear in direction. Thus disagreements and some degree of confusion are occurring, so that initial hopes and aspirations, the most important of which was that it would significantly reduce the number of offenders who had to be given custodial sentences, are to some extent being thwarted.

Part One

LEGISLATION AND PRACTICE

1

The background

Penal policy is not formulated in a vacuum, but neither is it necessarily the product of a coherent and consistent consensus. An adequate understanding of any changes or innovations in penal policy must therefore involve a historically informed appreciation of the situation, and of the sometimes conflicting pressures which confront policy-makers. Those pressures inevitably impose certain constraints, and dictate what is politically necessary on the one hand and politically feasible on the other. Although an innovation, the community service order was in several respects not a strong departure from the penal policy of the immediately preceding years; it was both a continuation and a culmination of it, emerging out of many different strands of opinion expressed by the Home Office, M.P.s, and interested pressure groups—both official and unofficial.

The most important pressure for change stemmed from the growing desire to divert offenders from custodial sentences. This is clearly reflected in the rapid proliferation over the last twenty years of innovations designed to restrict the use of imprisonment, to expand existing non-custodial measures, and to provide wholly new ones. The number of new measures introduced, particularly in the last decade or so, is both impressive and disquieting. Suspended sentences, parole, suspended sentence supervision orders, community service orders, day training centres, detoxification centres, bail hostels, the power to defer sentence, and the extension of existing resources such as probation hostels: all these provide evidence of mounting pressure to avoid imprisonment. Moreover, the power of magistrates to impose a prison sentence upon young adults, first offenders, and more recently those without a previous prison sentence, has been statutorily restricted to those for whom no other method is deemed appropriate.

However, non-custodial alternatives to imprisonment were not new phenomena: they had gradually developed during the last half of the nineteenth century and were well established by the first half of the twentieth.[1] Two immediate questions therefore arise. First, why was this sudden stimulus given to the trend away from confinement as a response to criminal behaviour? And secondly, what were the supposed defects of existing non-custodial measures which made it apparently so imperative that additional sentences be devised, and determined the form that they took?

The disillusion with imprisonment

The recent widespread disillusion with imprisonment as a penal sanction can be traced to four main themes in penal policy: the influence of humanitarianism; scepticism about the effectiveness of imprisonment as an instrument of treatment or a means of deterrence; prison overcrowding; and economic stringencies.[2] These factors, of course, overlap and interrelate, but they have not made an equal contribution to the impetus given to the development and use of non-custodial measures, as is evident when each is considered in turn.

First, while it is true that as social conditions have improved there has been a gradual but perceptible alteration of opinion on the minimum humanitarian standards appropriate for the administration of penal measures, in the last twenty years this has not been evident to a much greater degree than before. Likewise, while large institutions have increasingly come to be seen as unnatural and inhumane—and not just in the penal field—this has not been matched to any large extent by greater public tolerance for dealing with deviants in the community. An illustration of this is the local opposition often aroused by proposals for the setting up of hostels (see Home Office, 1976: para. 131; Greenberg, 1975: pp. 24–5). Indeed, alleged rises in the crime rate, particularly in crimes of violence, have often prompted the opposite reaction: demands for stronger security and harsher penalties, including longer prison sentences.

Secondly, the perception that imprisonment is ineffective, although clearly a dominant force in debates on penal policy since the 1950s, fails to explain adequately why non-custodial measures were proffered as an alternative.

Certainly, during the 1950s and 1960s sceptics were increasingly challenging the long-held assumption that imprisonment could be an effective deterrent to the individual upon whom it was imposed, while its regime could provide an effective rehabilitative environment. Initially they confined themselves to attacking short terms of imprisonment (e.g. Home Office, 1957; Scottish Home and Health Department, 1960). But during the 1960s the expressed confidence in long-term training also disappeared (e.g. Labour Party Study Group, 1964: p. 46; Conservative Party Study Group, 1966: p. 31; Home Office, 1965: para. 3). Thus the Wootton Committee, for example, viewed imprisonment as 'inappropriate and harmful for many offenders for whom it is used' (Home Office, 1970a: para. 8). By the time of the introduction of the community service order in 1972, a majority of Parliament seem to have finally rejected imprisonment as a reformative tool or an instrument of individual deterrence. Sir David Renton, the Under-Secretary of State for the Home Office, stated, 'What will distinguish the discussion on this Bill from previous discussions is doubt about the value of prison as such.' (H.C. Debates, 826: col. 990)

But what was so different about alternatives to custody? There was little empirical evidence to suggest that community-based measures would be any more successful than institutions in reducing recidivism. A growing number of research reports were producing consistently depressing conclusions.[3] Yet at the same time calls for the greater use of non-custodial measures continued unabated. Significantly, too, the possibility that imprisonment might be a general deterrent to other potential offenders was largely ignored in attacks on its effectiveness.

Moreover, it is important to consider what measure of relative efficacy was used in comparing custodial and non-custodial sentences. The Wootton Committee gave no indication of whether the community service order should be adjudged a success only if it produced lower recidivism rates than imprisonment, or merely rates that were no higher. But Lady Wootton, the Chairman of the Committee, later suggested that if 'it ever did turn out that the c.s.o. was *at least as successful a treatment* as imprisonment, judged by the rate of subsequent recidivism, for a substantial number of offenders' (my emphasis), then an expansion of the scheme to all parts of the country would be desirable (Wootton, 1973: pp. 19–20). This clearly indicates that recidivism was not the only criterion by which non-custodial measures were being assessed. They were apparently thought to possess other advantages over imprisonment, which at least served the additional function of keeping the offender out of circulation during his sentence. Thus the Government extended the community service scheme nation-wide before any evidence of reconviction rates had even become available.

The third theme—prison overcrowding—has also been a major preoccupation of post-war penal policy. There has been an inexorable rise in the population of penal establishments since 1948, increasing from a daily average population then of 19,318 to one of

31,984 in 1968; and this despite the fact that the number of immediate prison sentences passed, as a proportion of the total number
of sentences imposed on offenders convicted of indictable offences,
has steadily fallen during the same period.

Two factors contributed to this dramatic increase. First, there
was an enormous rise in the total number of persons convicted of
criminal offences, so that while the *proportion* of cases in which the
courts resorted to custodial sentences fell, the actual *number* of
receptions under sentence into penal establishments rose from
32,865 in 1948 to 49,258 in 1968. Secondly, it appears that there
was a slight increase in the length of prison sentences imposed. For
example, the proportion of prison sentences of over two years
imposed by higher courts rose from 15 per cent in 1948 to 26 per
cent in 1968.[4] This is probably partly attributable in itself to the
development of alternatives to short terms of imprisonment, and
partly to a change in the nature of crimes being dealt with. The
result was a vastly inflated prison population and chronically over-
crowded establishments.

Moreover, the restrictions on the use of imprisonment and the
development of non-custodial measures throughout the 1960s
and early 1970s did not seem to be having the desired effect. At the
most, they merely soaked up some of the increase in the crime rate.
Hence the problem of overcrowding remained a current concern.
The suspended sentence introduced in 1967 provides a case in
point. By 1972 it was commonly agreed that 'the suspended
sentence has been used more widely than was intended and also that
the sentences given have been longer' (H.C. Debates, 838: col.
1081). Apparently it had not proved an acceptable alternative to
imprisonment for the numbers intended. Moreover, there was a
suspicion that it had sometimes been activated upon breach in
circumstances where imprisonment would not previously have been
contemplated, thus indirectly increasing the numbers in prison.
Hence other ways of relieving overcrowding had to be found.

The compelling need to ease overburdened prison resources was
the yardstick used in Parliament to judge the provisions of the 1972
Criminal Justice Bill. Time and again in both Houses of Parliament
reference was made to the 'exploding prison population' and 'a
prison building programme which signally fails to keep up with that
population trend' (H.C. Debates, 826: col. 990). The Home Secretary, the late Reginald Maudling, in introducing the Second Reading
of the Bill, placed primary emphasis upon this point. He said:

> There has been an enormous increase in the prison population, which is
> about four times the size it was before the war. . . . The conditions in our

prisons are very serious. We must pay particular attention to this problem of overcrowding. . . . Thus the Bill embarks on a new range of noncustodial penalties designed to find methods of awarding punishments to criminals which do not involve incarcerating them. (H.C. Debates, 826: col. 966)

It was not simply humanitarianism or fears about the effect on rehabilitative objectives which prompted such widespread concern about the problem of overcrowding. It was described as 'the worst feature of our prison system' (Home Office, 1969: para. 239), not just because of its interference with treatment and training goals but because of its threat to security and its adverse effect on the morale of the prison service.

However, again this does not completely explain why noncustodial measures were seen as the remedy: the provision of new institutions would have been an alternative solution. There is nothing to suggest that projections of future population levels were inaccurate. In 1969, for example, the Home Office stated its belief that 'the prison service must plan on the assumption that the number of people in custody is likely to continue to rise by over 1,000 a year' (Home Office, 1969: para. 239), a prediction which has on average proved fairly accurate. Yet although there was an increase in capital expenditure on prisons, it was not sufficient to cater for this rise. Implicit in official policy has been the attitude that as the problem worsened, other non-custodial solutions would have to be found.

It thus seems clear that it is primarily the fourth influence on penal policy—financial considerations—that has given the search for alternatives to custody its cogency in the formulation of recent policy. Other factors have been important, but the need to restrict public expenditure has given them added weight. Of course, economy and expediency have always been central to policy-making, but their importance has been accentuated by the growth of the Welfare State and the increasing involvement of the State in industry and other spheres of public life, resulting in massive increases in State and local authority spending. Paradoxically, too, the augmentation of social service provision in the community, while leading to general budgetary strains, has also provided some of the community resources required for the handling of more offenders outside of prisons. Although community control and community care were in themselves becoming more and more costly, they nevertheless appeared to compare favourably with the financial costs of imprisonment. Predictably, therefore, community-based measures came to be seen as the panacea for the ills of prison overcrowding.

Cost was a significant factor in the debate on the First Offenders' Bill in 1958, the Joint Under-Secretary of State observing that 'it costs £6 11s [0.65p] a week of the taxpayers' money to keep a man in prison, and that cost should be avoided if possible' (H.C. Debates, 587: col. 754). An influential Labour Party group also mentioned the economic benefits of 'keeping people out of prison and productively employed' (Labour Party Study Group, 1964: pp. 42–3). The Wootton Committee saw prison as a wasteful use of resources. It continued:

> Cost is not the only factor, but it is worth observing that, quite apart from the increased risk that the State would have to support the family of an offender deprived of liberty, the cost of maintaining an inmate in prison service establishments is on the average about £22 a week. No official estimate has been made of the average cost of supervising a probationer but we would judge it to be of the order of £1 a week. (Home Office, 1970a: para. 9)

The Government, and pressure groups seeking penal reform, were usually more circumspect; economic motives remained largely unstated in the parliamentary debates of the 1960s and 1970s. Nevertheless, they were the driving force behind concerns about prison overcrowding, prison ineffectiveness, and simple humanitarianism. The economic strictures explain the susceptibility of penal policy to the influence of other arguments which were not in themselves sufficient to explain the disillusion with imprisonment.

The search for additional non-custodial measures

The mere fact that there was disillusionment with imprisonment does not explain why additional non-custodial measures were developed. It might have been possible instead simply to persuade courts to make more use of existing sentences. For example, although the Advisory Council on the Treatment of Offenders in 1957 encouraged the greater use of non-custodial measures, the only innovatory sentence that they proposed was the very minor extension of attendance centres to young adult offenders (Home Office, 1957).[5] In the main, they appeared to accept that existing measures, if properly used, were quite adequate.

During the 1960s, however, the situation changed. The belief that new sentences should be devised, and the pressures that influenced the form they took, stemmed directly from the growth in recorded crime and the number of convicted offenders, and from the failure of current penal measures to curtail them. The reorganization and extension of the whole field of social insurance and allied social services after the Second World War had been accompanied by a pervasive mood of optimism, which encompassed all features of the social system. Admittedly there was some anxiety, for example, about juvenile crime in the immediate post-war period, but none the less the Utopian ideal of social reconstruction had few opponents. The apparatus of the Welfare State was directed towards those features of society that formed the basis of popular theories of crime causation: poverty, poor housing conditions, lack of education and employment opportunities, and class conflict. Thus it was not unreasonable to expect a reduction in the crime rate. This hope seemed to be confirmed by the fact that the statistics for crime remained fairly constant between 1948 and 1957, and even dropped slightly after 1953.

However, the late 1950s and the 1960s witnessed the apparent failure of social welfare measures in this respect. Despite over-all prosperity, by 1966 the proportion of offenders found guilty of indictable offences per head of population was more than double the 1956 level and penal policy seemed unable to contain it. At one extreme, the 'anti-collectivists' blamed the Welfare State. Some Conservatives—Enoch Powell being one such example— argued that the Welfare State had promoted the disruption of the social fabric and the abrogation of personal responsibility. It was alleged that the conversion of an individual need or want into a social right had resulted in the State having become both the source and focus of social and personal grievances. At the other extreme, it was maintained that social welfare had not yet gone far enough; that 'poverty, squalor and social inadequacy still exist on a considerable scale' (Labour Party Study Group, 1964: p. 4).

Whatever view was taken, earlier optimism was tempered by the realities of the situation; the causes of crime might be too complex to be overcome solely by the Utopian solutions of the Welfare State. That is not to say that its ideals were necessarily thought misplaced: it was merely a recognition that earlier claims were at least rather too simplistic.

It was thus predictable that the existing non-custodial measures —chiefly the fine, the probation order, and the discharge—were no longer thought appropriate for every situation in which a non-custodial option might be contemplated. Although the proportionate use of the fine—which had remained fairly constant throughout the 1950s—increased slightly in the first half of the 1960s, the difficulties of fine enforcement, and the possibility that fine defaulters would further swell the prison population, depreciated its value. It is significant that greater restrictions in s.44 of the Criminal Justice Act 1967 upon the power of magistrates to commit fine defaulters to prison proved controversial. Not only was there opposition from M.P.s, the Magistrates' Association, and the Justices' Clerks' Society (Softley, 1973: p. 1), but the City Magistrates' Court at Manchester submitted a memorandum to the Parliamentary Standing Committee, attacking it as a further encroachment upon their powers to impose effective penalties (H.C. Debates, Standing Committee A, 28/2/67: col. 600).

There was also a questioning of the global objectives of the probation service and other personal social services. It is true that traditional approaches to rehabilitation, which utilized the principles of social casework and by and large concentrated upon the problems of the offender, were not abandoned during the 1960s. Indeed, the probation service was expanded to take over a general responsibility for after-care and prison welfare. However, there were at this time the first signs of a realistic reappraisal of how far this method could hope to alter people's attitudes. Barbara Wootton, for example, stated her belief that 'the social worker's best, indeed perhaps her only, chance of achieving [the] aims [of traditional casework] . . . would be to marry her client' (Wootton, 1959: p. 273). Moreover, there was some small evidence that the probation order was not as effective as had been hoped: according to a study by Hammond in 1957, probationers fared considerably worse in terms of recidivism than those upon whom fines and discharges were imposed (Home Office, 1964: paras 157 ff.).[6] It is thus worth noting that a consequence of the introduction of the suspended sentence in 1967 was an immediate decline in the use of the probation order.

Whatever the appropriateness, therefore, of the existing non-custodial measures for the offenders upon whom they were at that time imposed, it could not be expected that their use as alternatives to custodial sentences would be greatly extended. If a reduction in the use of imprisonment was really to be achieved, new non-custodial approaches would have to be found. The form that these approaches took was determined by three groups of pressures: demands for stronger penalties; calls for more attention to the needs of victims; and an emphasis upon reintegration and community involvement as a means of rehabilitation.

a. The demand for sterner penalties

The appeals for harsher non-custodial measures were a natural consequence of the rise in the crime rate and the intention to reduce the proportion of offenders incarcerated. There were general fears that too little attention was being paid to deterrence and protection of the public, and some resentment that criminals were getting off too lightly. Thus the introduction of non-custodial measures with some 'teeth' to them was the price to be paid for the decreasing use of custody.

Such penal bargaining is, of course, common to most accounts of changes or innovations in penal policy. For example, the detention centre order, introduced in the Criminal Justice Act 1948 with the avowed intention of administering a short sharp shock to young hooligans, was in part a response to the formal abolition of the birch in the same Act. In 1938 the Cadogan Committee, which recommended that corporal punishment be abolished, had suggested that there was nevertheless a need for 'some form of short and sharp punishment' to pull up the minor juvenile offender and 'give him the lesson which he needs' (Departmental Committee on Corporal Punishment, 1938: p 46). It was quite evident by 1948 that the abolition of the birch was a viable proposition only if something relatively severe and explicitly deterrent were put in its place. The detention centre order served that function. A similar example is the mandatory life sentence for murder which emerged as a result of the abolition of the death penalty for murder in 1965.

A penal policy which heeded calls for a stronger punitive or deterrent element in non-custodial sentences, therefore, was essentially a political expedient designed to encourage the use of non-custodial measures at a time when there was public concern about the volume of crime. One practical expression of it was the introduction of the suspended sentence in 1967. Its political appeal was reflected in the fact that, although the Wootton Committee had been charged in November 1966 with the specific task of considering changes in and additions to non-custodial penalties, the Government deemed it unnecessary to await its report. This is the more remarkable because in 1957 the idea had been rejected as 'wrong in principle and to a large extent impracticable' (Home Office, 1957: para. 23). It was obvious that the view expressed then that existing measures provided sufficient alternatives to imprisonment, was no longer politically tenable. It is true that the suspended sentence was not a severe measure in itself; only the commission of a further offence could make it so. Nevertheless, the explicit threat of imprisonment gave it a certain symbolic severity and a distinctly deterrent flavour which fitted in nicely with demands for stronger penalties. Looked at in this way, it is not surprising that it came to be used as an alternative to both the fine and probation order as well as imprisonment.

b. The needs of the victim

Another manifestation of the reaction against apparent leniency and too much concern for the needs and welfare of the criminal was the view that the offender should be compelled to make amends for his actions by some form of reparation to the victim. Though there were scattered provisions for this, for instance in conjunction with a probation order or a discharge under s.11 of the Criminal Justice Act 1948, they were very little used. A common theme of informed opinion was the injustice of penal policy in allowing criminals to 'get away with it' while victims were left to suffer.[7] In 1957, for example, Margery Fry suggested a scheme of State compensation for victims of crimes of violence (Fry, 1957), although there was no suggestion that it should involve a contribution from the offenders themselves.[8] In the same year the Advisory Council on the Treatment of Offenders suggested that there might be greater scope for ordering compensation and restitution than was then allowed (Home Office, 1957: para. 62). In 1959 the White Paper *Penal Practice in a Changing Society* (Home Office, 1959) was the first official document to take up the suggestion that a change in approach might be desirable in order to provide a better balance between the needs of offenders and the needs of victims. Moreover, it included the surmise that this might be of benefit to offenders as well as to victims by making them realize the damage or injury they had caused.

During the 1960s the idea of personal reparation received more widespread attention. In particular, it was mentioned by various bodies in evidence presented to the Royal Commission on the Penal System. The Magistrates' Association advocated that courts be given a general power to order compensation by the offender to the victim (Royal Commission on the Penal System, 1967a: vol. II, para. 68). The evidence of the Justices' Clerks' Society was more specific:

> . . . we suggest an exploration of the possibility of making an offender do something to put right, quite personally, and in a practical way, the loss or damage he has caused by his offence. We have in mind, for example, the provision of powers enabling courts to order a person dropping litter to sweep the streets, or those committing damage to assist in effecting the repairs, and so on. (Ibid.: vol. II, para. 15)

Throughout the 1960s several individuals[9] also proposed that community work be used as a form of reparation, either directly to victims or more generally to society against which the criminal had allegedly offended.

A direct outcome of these general views was the appointment of a sub-committee of the Advisory Council on the Penal System under the chairmanship of Lord Widgery 'to consider how the principle of personal reparation might be given a more prominent place in the penal system' (Home Office, 1970b: p. v). The Committee stated that 'it is the philosophy of remedying the specific consequences of the offence which seems to us to underlie the general plea for greater emphasis on reparation' (ibid.: para. 2). They clearly felt that the offender should no longer be allowed to evade his responsibilities and cause loss, damage, or injury with apparent financial impunity. As a result of their recommendations, therefore, the Criminal Justice Act 1972 made more general the court's power to order compensation and restitution, and introduced criminal bankruptcy orders.

c. Reintegration and community involvement
Despite the demand for greater severity in non-custodial sanctions, there also existed a lobby advocating a greater diversity in rehabilitative methods. It was a matter of finding the right balance between deterrence and treatment. The one which appeared to offer the most promise was a 'reintegrative model': the offender should be dealt with in the context of his community, and the community should be involved in the rehabilitative effort, thus enabling the offender to be reconciled to the society from which his offending had alienated him.

The reintegrative perspective must, of course, be seen in the social and political context in which penal policy was being formulated. One response to the failure of social welfare provisions to solve the problem of an accelerating crime rate was a greater emphasis upon personal responsibility. As a corollary, importance was attached to the reciprocal obligations of members of a community. The malaise of present-day society was often perceived in terms of the breakdown of social cohesion and the growing impersonality of social interaction. The Conservative Party Study Group stated it in these terms:

> In the impersonal society, concepts such as 'the public good' and 'social well-being' tend to lose their significance. Motives frequently become selfish and community values and loyalties diminish in their influence. (Conservative Party Study Group, 1966: p. 15)

State involvement in the solution of social ills, therefore, was not enough; there had to be individual participation and help in meeting social problems. Crime prevention was seen as the direct responsibility of the community, and the integration of the offender with the community as the most promising means of attack on crime. The imposition of a comprehensive social service bureaucracy had not produced consensus and social cohesion. Indeed, some welfare measures—rehousing, for example—had seemingly produced the opposite effect: the breakdown of community spirit and 'alienation between the authority and people' (Ministry of Housing, 1969: p. 3). There was therefore a vague hope that the participation of individual citizens in the problems of the community might engender some community spirit from within.

These appeals to individual responsibility were undoubtedly a reaction against the impersonality of urban materialistic society. They were thus an attempt to pierce the façade of superficiality and indifference which was graphically described in the Albemarle Report:

> We do not think it is easy or wise to speak glibly of a delinquent younger generation or a law-abiding older generation. This is only half the story. What, to a person of forty or fifty may show itself as a general malaise, a sense of emptiness, a quiet rejection of social responsibilities or a cautiously controlled cynicism, may show itself in an adolescent as an act of wanton violence, a bout of histrionic drunkenness or a grasping at promiscuous sexual experience. There does not seem to be at the heart of society a courageous and exciting struggle for a particular moral and spiritual life—only a passive neutral commitment to things as they are. One cannot, in fact, indict the young for the growth of delinquency without also indicting the older generations for apathy and indifference to the deeper things of the heart. (Ministry of Education, para. 63)

In these appeals there was no attempt to contrast city and country or factory and farm. Rather, it was a distinction between responsibility and irresponsibility, altruism and selfishness, participation and anonymity.

The belief that a sense of social responsibility and altruism needed to be injected into society by the involvement of its members in each other's problems and needs was directly applicable to penal policy. It was axiomatic that the criminal trial and conviction involved stereotyping and stigmatization. It was believed that as a result the criminal justice process often perpetuated or reinforced the offender's estrangement from the community. Not only that, but rehabilitative measures such as the probation order tended to encourage this by focusing on the offender's deviance and problems rather than his normality and positive attributes. So a penal policy was needed which had as one of its objectives the reconciliation of the offender and the community; instead of confirming deviant identities and roles, it should seek the means to change them and render them less important. As a Working Party on voluntary service in after-care stated:

> Discharged offenders need to live in a society which accepts them back into its midst with equal rights. . . . It is important that the stereotype of the discharged offender should be removed and that the public should be encouraged to appreciate that a prisoner who has completed his sentence must return to society and be accepted as an individual. (Home Office, 1967: para. 6)

Essentially, then, a reintegrative penal model involved 'delabelling': the restoration of the offender to a position of worth in society by his involvement in the community and the community's involvement with him.

One medium through which this emphasis upon community involvement found practical expression was the voluntary service movement. Voluntary agencies, of course, had existed for centuries to alleviate the worst excesses of poverty, want, and disease. But following the comprehensive social service legislation of the 1940s, voluntary organizations in fact flourished and expanded rather than declined.

There was good reason for this. Voluntary agencies had certain advantages over their statutory counterparts. First, they were more flexible and therefore far better equipped to experiment, follow up new ideas, and act in controversial matters, than State services could ever be. Secondly, they could serve to highlight needs which had hitherto gone unnoticed. Thirdly, they could act as a corrective to the possible inertia and complacency of the statutory service bureaucracy. Finally, in reality statutory social services could not hope to provide adequately for all needs in every case; voluntary service was therefore an essential supplement.

The continued existence of voluntary agencies thus provided a ready outlet for appeals to individual responsibility and calls for personal involvement in the meeting of community needs. Voluntary service, in the formal sense, had traditionally been the domain of the middle classes, who had spare leisure time, a sense of commitment, and were spurred on by their social consciences. But as the Seebohm Committee argued, voluntary service was seen not merely as a duty but as a means of personal fulfilment, participation, and sharing, and of encouraging 'informal "good neighbourliness"' (Committee on Local Authority and Allied Personal Social Services, 1968: para. 497). By its extension to all sectors of the population, the sense of community spirit, which had declined with the break-up of working-class neighbourhoods, might be recreated.

Moreover, it was hoped that if voluntary service were practised more widely, the gap might be bridged between givers and takers: between the dispensers of material welfare on the one hand and its recipients on the other. The Seebohm Committee suggested that a pressure was making itself felt for the involvement of people themselves in determining and meeting their own and others' needs. It went on:

> The development of citizen participation should reduce the rigid distinction between the givers and the takers of social services and the stigma which being a client has often involved in the past. (ibid.: para. 492).

The ideology of voluntary service was also seen to have particular application to the problems of youth. Many of the social changes of the post-war period seemed to have had their most marked effect on adolescents. The increased stress on consumption rather than production in the affluent society produced what became known as 'the teenage consumer', whose spending power had expanded at twice the rate of adults (Abrams, 1959: p. 9). The Conservative Party Study Group (1966: p. 14) and the Albemarle Report (Ministry of Education, 1960: paras 89–99) both referred to the development of commercial interests specifically designed to exploit this spending power; the existing means of utilizing the full variety and potentiality of teenagers' interests were outdated and unappealing, so that adolescents merely earned and consumed. This, combined with greater mobility and more leisure, was believed to be creating alienation and irresponsibility:

> The first of [the reasons for the growing importance of leisure] is the emancipation of the adolescent, happening so suddenly that it has taken everybody by surprise. Young people nowadays have more surplus energy than they have ever had before—and all within the space of a decade. What all too many of them lack, however, is a corresponding sense of purpose and of personal responsibility. (Conservative Political Centre, 1959: p. 5)

Voluntary service could provide a means of counteracting this trend and perhaps of realizing the latent altruism of youth. Thus the appeals to community spirit were of particular relevance to young people; voluntary service was an ideal means of channelling their energies for constructive ends and allowing them an opportunity to give. At the same time it could inculcate a sense of community responsibility and break down the impersonality of modern society.

It is hardly surprising, therefore, that voluntary service by young people was given a boost during the 1960s. On a general level the opportunity was extended in many areas to young people still at school; previously it had usually been available to this age group only through membership of organizations such as the Scouts. More importantly, Voluntary Service Overseas, set up in 1958 to enable school-leavers, cadets, and apprentices aged 17 to 20 to serve full time for a limited period in areas of need overseas, was extended in 1962 by the establishment of Community Service Volunteers (C.S.V.) to allow full-time service in England. It was argued that the sense of responsibility and fulfilment that young people could achieve by serving their own communities was just as important as the glamour of overseas service. C.S.V. were particularly concerned to pioneer new projects. Their first pamphlet ended with these words:

> This endeavour is concerned not just to place candidates in projects— but to explore new patterns of service, to expand the role of the volunteer in society, and to discover what contribution the young can make to the care of the community. (cited in Community Service Volunteers Annual Report, 1966–7: p. 1)

C.S.V. also quickly became involved in advising people on how to undertake local community service, and in participating in the extension of voluntary service in schools.

These sentiments underlying the expansion of voluntary service were obviously of particular relevance to a reintegrative penal model. Community involvement; the reduction of stigma; the concentration upon positive attributes and altruism; the special focus on providing outlets for the talents of youth: all these were crucial to the effective reintegration of offenders within the community. In fact, the involvement of offenders in voluntary service, albeit informally and sporadically, even preceded the general expansion of the voluntary service movement. Informal arrangements had been afoot for some time between prison governors and certain local communities for the employment of adult prisoners on a voluntary basis in community work. Later voluntary organizations acted as the channel for such work. For instance, from 1960 to 1965 International Voluntary Service arranged for volunteer prisoners from Wandsworth Prison to carry out community service tasks in association with non-offender volunteers. Of even more direct relevance was the involvement of *young* offenders in the performance of voluntary service: since before the Second World War, Borstals had been releasing trainees for voluntary work in local communities.

During the 1960s such informal arrangements became more widespread, as approved schools, detention centres, and Borstals began to release inmates for a week or longer, towards the end of their sentences, to work full time as ordinary volunteers—usually in an institution such as a home for the mentally handicapped. This was sometimes done through C.S.V.: by the late 1960s approved schools and Scottish Borstals were releasing trainees during their sentences to C.S.V. for work as full-time volunteers. In 1971 the Home Office granted permission for Borstal trainees in England to be seconded to C.S.V. for the same purpose during the final two or three months of their sentences.[10] By the end of 1975 there were ten Borstals participating in this scheme with up to 100 boys involved at any one time. The C.S.V. Borstal programme in England was, of course, too late to influence the idea of the community service order. Nevertheless, it indicates that voluntary service was one of the current bandwagons in penal policy.

During the 1960s there was also growing interest in voluntary work by offenders subject to non-custodial measures. The probation service, for example, began to arrange placements for clients with voluntary organizations during the 1960s—again on an entirely voluntary basis. In 1965, Richard Hauser suggested in evidence to the Royal Commission on the Penal System that it could be a valuable means of:

> fostering a sense of responsibility among young offenders for each other. For the socially inadequate, crime is a creative outlet. Those who are active in it to prove their ability should be used as leaders to help with a positive response to the needs of the community, whereas now their energies are completely wasted, on what are largely crimes of boredom. (Royal Commission on the Penal System, 1967b: p. 11)

The introduction of the community service order

The idea of the community service order owed much to all these pressures. Unarguably it was designed to serve, at least in part, as an alternative to custodial sentences. Although the original terms of reference simply required the Wootton Committee 'to consider what changes and additions might be made to the existing range of non-custodial penalties, disabilities, and other requirements which may be imposed on offenders', it saw its primary task as devising alternatives to custodial sentences (Home Office, 1970a: para. 4). In recommending the community service order, it expressed the 'hope that an obligation to perform community service would be felt by the courts to constitute an adequate alternative to a short custodial sentence', although it did not want to preclude its use in other cases where it might be thought more appropriate than existing non-custodial sanctions (ibid.: para. 37).

The Government was firmer in its resolve that it should operate primarily to divert offenders from custody. The Home Secretary stated in Parliament:

> I was attracted from the start to the idea that people who have committed minor offences would be better occupied doing a service to their fellow citizens than sitting alongside others in a crowded gaol. (H.C. Debates, 826: col. 972)

This, however, had an element of exaggeration characteristic of political rhetoric. A more sober version of the Government's policy was later given by the Under-Secretary, Mr Carlisle, during the Committee stage:

> We hope . . . that the courts will look upon this as an adequate and suitable alternative to the short custodial sentence. Therefore, we hope that it will keep out of prison some people who now go there. . . . I am not for the moment suggesting that in future everyone will receive a sentence of community service where previously he would have received a custodial sentence. I believe that it will be used where people are now dealt with in other non-custodial ways. However, I hope that courts will be encouraged also to use it in place of short custodial sentences. (H.C. Debates, Standing Committee G, 8/2/72: cols 472–3)

The view that community service should operate primarily, although not exclusively, as an alternative to imprisonment, was echoed by the Home Office on two subsequent occasions: first, in a publication intended to be a brief introduction for the courts to the Criminal Justice Act 1972 (Home Office, 1972: p. 10); and secondly, in a circular in 1974 to probation areas setting up new schemes (Home Office Circular no. 197/1974: p. 8). It was also reiterated in a speech by the Lord Chancellor to the Magistrates' Association in 1976.[11]

The Government's commitment to the community service order as a viable alternative to a short custodial sentence directly resulted in three significant departures from the Wootton Committee proposals in the Criminal Justice Bill prepared for Parliament in 1972. All served to emphasize the penal content of the sentence and were designed to make it more attractive to sentencers.

First, whereas the Committee had suggested that community service would be a useful penalty for certain non-imprisonable traffic offences, the Government instead adopted the advice of a Working Group of officials set up by the Home Office to consider the feasibility of community service, and restricted the sentence to offences punishable by imprisonment. This was designed to stress the position that they expected it to occupy in the scale of penalties.

Secondly, the legislation substantially altered the number of hours' work that an order could impose. The Wootton Committee had suggested a maximum of 120 hours, and did not recommend any minimum. The Home Office Working Group, while supporting a maximum of 120 hours, considered that an order of less than forty might appear trivial. The Government not only decided on a minimum of forty hours but also doubled the proposed maximum to 240. The reason was clear:

> The Home Office felt that if the courts were to be encouraged to use this as an alternative to short custodial sentences, a maximum of 120 hours was too little and the courts would be more likely to look on it as an alternative to the custodial sentence if they could order fairly substantial hours of work to be done. (H.C. Debates, Standing Committee G, 8/2/72: col. 473)

Against this it was suggested that the Wootton Committee proposals were more suitable for an experiment, as a period of 240 hours opened the way to non-co-operation and failure (Fraser, H.C. Debates, 838: col. 1964). However, the Government remained firm in its resolve: courts should have as much flexibility as possible in imposing the required degree of punishment; the community service order was not to be regarded as another 'soft option'.

Finally, the Wootton Committee had discussed at length whether the community service order should be a separate sentence of the court or merely a requirement of a probation order. Its final solution was clearly a compromise. Some of the members of the Committee had felt that, at least during the experimental period, an extension to the framework of probation would be easier administratively, as it would utilize an established procedure in cases of breach. Not only would it give the probation service more room to manoeuvre, but it would also provide the machinery for support and supervision should this be necessary. Against this, others in the Committee had pointed out that many of the offenders suitable for community service would not require probation supervision at all, and that its exclusive association with probation might cause sentencers to regard it as a means of giving teeth to a probation order. In the end, it had been recommended that a compromise solution—giving an option to the court in each case—should be adopted.

However, the Government rejected this compromise, sharing the view of the officials of the Working Group that community service by order of the court was a new and separate concept in the treatment of offenders, and as such merited an independent position among the courts' sanctions and, accordingly, should be a sentence quite distinct from the probation order. Presumably it was believed that linking it to probation would have jeopardized its position as an alternative to custody for offenders for whom probation might be regarded as too mild a measure.

The idea of the community service order was thus firmly rooted in the search for alternatives to custody. It was a politically expedient measure introduced in the light of a need for an urgent reduction in the prison population. That was the reason for the rapid translation into legislation of some of the recommendations of the Wootton Committee in such a comparatively short time. As the Shadow Home Secretary commented, some of the members of the Committee must have been 'gratified and a little surprised to see their proposals translated into a Bill only eighteen months after they reported. In some ways, that is a little unusual' (H.C. Debates, 826: col. 979). The fact that the community service order was essentially a political expedient had two important consequences.

The first of these was the largely unquestioned acceptance of the prevailing belief that new non-custodial measures were necessary. Thus there was no systematic examination of the reasons why courts were not using existing non-custodial measures enough; there was simply a belief that they lacked sufficient flexibility and diversity. Although it was admitted that greater use of existing powers was possible, the Committee presumed that the most promising line was to consider what new non-custodial penalties were required if offenders who at present went to prison were to be dealt with non-custodially. The fact that existing measures were too little used was in itself seen as evidence of the need for innovation.

The Advisory Council on the Treatment of Offenders (the forerunner of the Advisory Council on the Penal System) had asserted that a proposal for change should be accompanied by reasons why 'the suggested innovation would be a positive improvement on existing methods' (Home Office, 1957: para. 9). This advice was forgotten or ignored by the Wootton Committee, which was clearly at fault, as Lady Wootton has since recognized, 'in not developing more fully the reasons for the choice of [its] particular hypothesis' (Wootton, 1977: p. 19). It would not, of course, have been possible to predict whether the community service order would be effective in reducing recidivism; only *post hoc* evaluation could indicate that. But the Committee did not even attempt to set out the reasons for which sentencers sometimes rejected existing non-custodial measures, nor why the community service order might be more attractive to them. It simply said, rather weakly:

We have not attempted to categorize precisely the types of offenders for whom community service might be appropriate, nor do we think it possible to predict what use might be made by the courts of this new form of sentence. (Home Office, 1970a: para. 37)

Yet, unless the new sentence appealed to sentencers as a viable alternative to custody, its main point would be missed.

Of course, it is true that well developed notions were available about the defects of existing measures and the Committee implicitly relied on these. The second consequence of the political expediency of the measure, therefore, was a totally uncritical acceptance of the concept of community service by offenders, both by the Wootton Committee and later by Members of Parliament. Thus statements on its philosophy were vague and deliberately ambivalent. The Committee stated:

> The proposition that some offenders should be required to undertake community service should appeal to different varieties of penal philosophy. To some, it would be simply a more constructive and cheaper alternative to imprisonment; by others it would be seen as introducing into the penal system a new dimension with an emphasis on reparation to the community; others again would regard it as giving effect to the old adage that the punishment should fit the crime; while still others would stress the value of bringing offenders into close touch with those members of the community who are most in need of help and support. (Home Office, 1970a: para. 33)

Presumably it was felt that the success of the scheme would be assured by making it all things to all men; in other words, by making it cater as far as possible for all of the current pressures for change in penal policy.

It is likely, too, that the Committee's concentration upon the practical details of the scheme, to the virtual exclusion of matters relating to penal philosophy, arose from the fact that there was little agreement either inside or outside the Committee on questions of penal philosophy. Thus, instead of becoming bogged down, as the Royal Commission on the Penal System had earlier done, in debating issues of penal philosophy or risking the possibility that political divisiveness on tendentious theoretical issues would endanger the practical acceptability of the proposals, the Committee preferred to follow Radzinowicz's earlier advice to accept 'diversity in the purposes of punishment' (Radzinowicz, 1966: p. 115).

Hood (1974) criticized the Committee's proposal for the community service order, on the grounds that it was based upon an ideology. Clearly, however, it is more accurate and relevant to claim that it was designed to appeal to a range of differing ideologies, reflecting the considerations of expediency upon which the proposal was founded. In particular, it was linked, both by the Wootton Committee and by Members of Parliament in discussing the provisions of the Bill, to the need for sterner penalties, for measures with an explicitly reparative element, and for a new approach to rehabilitation. The Under-Secretary of State during the Committee stage of the Bill stated:

> Mr Silkin has asked how the Government saw the idea of community service fitting into the over-all penal policy. Did we look upon it as punitive or reformative? . . . My answer would be that any form of sentence which is available to the courts must surely try to achieve all the aims of sentencing, namely, to be punitive, reformative and preventative all at the same time. (H.C. Debates, Standing Committee G, 8/2/72: cols 472–3)

The sentence was regarded as punitive by depriving the offender of his free time and placing an obligation upon him to work; and reparative in requiring him to reimburse society for his crime by performing useful work. The allegedly reparative element, therefore, was not directed at the individual victim, as were the provisions of the Act for compensation orders, but at society in general.

The sentence was also clearly imbued with the general ethos of voluntary service and as a consequence was believed to be a means of reintegrating the offender with the community. The Wootton Committee was greatly influenced by this. Other possibilities, such as work parties on large-scale outdoor projects (e.g. reclaiming marshland) or work directly related to the nature of the offence (e.g. traffic offenders working in casualty wards of hospitals), were rejected in favour of community work of the type ordinarily undertaken by voluntary agencies. The idea of using work as a penalty or a means of rehabilitation was, of course, a very old one. In both capacities it had formed an important element of the regimes of prisons and Houses of Correction as far back as the sixteenth century, and, in the penal sense, had earlier found expression in other practices such as slavery. Yet curiously no direct reference was made to this in the discussions leading up to the community service order. Instead, the emphasis was placed upon the concept of voluntary service and the development of voluntary organizations.

The Committee also had described to it the New Zealand periodic detention work schemes, which incorporated community service activity with a system of week-end residential or non-residential attendance at a periodic detention centre.[12] In particular, they were told that, in small rural areas in New Zealand where the population did not warrant the setting up of a centre, the practice was to sentence offenders to a term of probation, a condition of which was that for some specified period and specified number of hours each week they should undertake special community work as the probation officer directed. The Committee's proposal bore close resemblance to this.

The Committee did not attempt to link the proposal to any notions of the causes of crime, and did not specify the mechanism by which community service might rehabilitate. However, it was undoubtedly believed to have the potential for rehabilitation by bringing the offender *qua* offender into direct contact with other members of the community, thereby effecting a 'reconciliation' between him and authority, from which he was usually alienated (H.C. Debates, 838: col. 1964). More specifically, it was suggested in Parliament that community service might achieve reintegration in two ways.

First, the offender would be placed in situations that would highlight his selfishness and would perhaps appeal to a latent sense of responsibility and altruism. This might act as a valuable counter to irresponsibility and short-term hedonism. By being obliged to help those in need, offenders might realize their duty to others in the community and at the same time show others that they were willing and able to contribute to society. Beliefs of this kind strongly influenced the Wootton Committee. Lady Wootton herself commented:

> I should like also to say that something of this kind on a voluntary basis is already being done with offenders. Some probationers are doing it at the instigation of their probation officers, and doing it quite happily and successfully, and in some open Borstals, young men are going to give service to the community, as for instance, in Cheshire Homes where they help to bath totally disabled people. It is found that the sight of persons far more disadvantaged than they are themselves, and the opportunity of helping such people, has a very beneficial effect on their attitudes. It is that kind of thing that we are thinking of in making these proposals. (H.L. Debates, 332: col. 611)

Secondly, it was emphasized that the scheme should allow as much scope as possible for work to be performed in association with non-offender volunteers, so that, in the words of the Wootton Committee, they could be subject to 'the wholesome influence of those who choose to engage voluntarily in these tasks' (Home Office, 1970a: para. 35). It was apparently assumed that the example of other volunteers might induce a change in the offender's outlook on society.

Since voluntary service was regarded as particularly relevant to the needs of youth, the community service order was correspondingly seen to be especially appropriate for young adult offenders. While the young adult offender was typically characterized as irres- ponsible, defiant of authority, and selfish, it was also recognized that he had potential to be utilized, and it was believed that he could re-establish himself in society if given the opportunity to help others. Moreover, he was regarded as more susceptible to peer group influences than an older offender, and thus more likely to benefit from the example of other young volunteers. Hence the Wootton Committee concluded that community service might be 'particularly valuable in the treatment of the young offender' (Home Office, 1970a: para. 38), although it was not of course restricted to that age group.

Many diverse pressures that affected penal policy during the 1950s and 1960s thus found expression in the community service order. In the first place, it was intended to operate mainly as an alternative to custody. Statutorily, however, it was limited to offences which *could* receive imprisonment, not (as in the case of the suspended sentence) to offenders who otherwise would have been imprisoned. In practice the Government did not want to exclude its use in other cases where sentencers might require more effective punishment, reparation, or rehabilitation. A scheme was therefore devised which could and did appeal to protagonists of many different, and sometimes conflicting, philosophical perspec- tives. As I will show later, this pragmatic acceptance of various philosophies and functions, and their attempted fusion within one sentence, has been perpetuated by the courts and the probation and after-care service. As a consequence, confusion and ambiguity have continued over the purpose of the sentence and the type of offender for which it is appropriate.

2

The legislation

The provisions of the Criminal Justice Act 1972 that introduced the community service order have been largely consolidated in and superseded by the Powers of Criminal Courts Act 1973.[1] The essential legal features of the scheme are contained in ss. 14–17 of that Act, as amended by Schedule 12 of the Criminal Law Act 1977.

To be eligible for the sentence, an offender must be aged 17 and over and have been convicted of an offence punishable by imprisonment. An order may be imposed by a Crown Court, a magistrates' court, or a juvenile court if the offender is 17 at the time of sentence. Before an order can be made, however, the court must consider a probation officer's report about the offender and his circumstances (although in practice reports by Social Services Departments on offenders subject to care orders are accepted in lieu), and must be satisfied as to the availability of suitable tasks in the area in which the offender resides. Moreover, it must explain the requirements and effect of the order to the offender and then obtain his consent to it. Orders imposed at any one court hearing must not total less than forty nor more than 240 hours in aggregate. Whether or not consecutive orders imposed at different court hearings may leave an outstanding obligation upon an offender of more than 240 hours, however, remains uncertain, although it appears from the wording of the legislation that they can.[2]

An offender subject to an order is required to report to the community service organizer as instructed, to notify him of any change of address, and to perform the number of hours' work specified in the order at the time and in the manner that he is instructed.

An offender thus cannot necessarily choose the times at which the work is done, and it is not uncommon for a court to impose an order on a football hooligan upon the informal understanding that he will be instructed to perform community service work on Saturday afternoons. However, work instructions have to avoid as far as possible any interference with work, educational, or religious activities.

The work is supposed to be performed within twelve months from the date of the order, unless an extension of time is granted by the court upon application by the offender or the community service organizer. Failure to complete within that period places the offender in breach of the order. The absence of breach proceedings by the organizer, however, does not allow the order to lapse; by virtue of the Criminal Law Act 1977 it continues in force until the required number of hours' work are completed, or until the order is revoked.

If an offender is proved to be in breach of any requirement of a community service order, he may be fined up to £50 and the order continued, or alternatively, the order may be revoked and he may be given any sentence which he could have received for the original offence. This is similar to the procedure for dealing with breach of a probation order or a conditional discharge, except that, unlike those sentences, a further offence does not of itself constitute a breach of a community service order.

There is also a further procedure by which the court, upon application by the offender or the community service organizer, can revoke an order in the interests of justice and impose any other sentence which could have been given for the original offence. Apart from obvious circumstances such as intervening ill health which make fulfilment of the order impossible, this provision is also commonly invoked following the imposition for a further offence of a custodial sentence, the length of which makes it unlikely that the order will be completed during the twelve-month period.

The requirement of consent

Why is the offender's consent to the making of a community service order required? An offender's consent to a probation order has always been required, following the tradition of the recognizance from which it stemmed. A probation order is imposed on an offender as a treatment measure 'instead of sentencing him' (s.2(1) Powers of Criminal Courts Act 1973), and renders the offender liable, upon breach of the order, to sentencing for the original offence. Consent is required both because a probation order is thought to be ineffective in the case of a totally uncooperative offender, and because it might be thought ethically objectionable to impose an alternative to a sentence upon an offender without his consent.

It is arguable that these reasons do not apply in respect of the community service order, and that consent is fundamentally inappropriate, especially in cases where the sentence is being used as an alternative to custody. There is an argument (used also in relation to the probation order) which disputes that consent can be valid in such circumstances, dismissing it as unreal and meaningless because coerced. However, this is confused thinking: coercion does not arise merely because the alternative is less attractive.

The community service order, unlike the probation order, is not an alternative to a sentence. In that sense it is more analogous to a fine than a probation order, and may be regarded as a penalty. The real question is whether consent is necessary or appropriate for such a measure. There are several cogent reasons why it is.

First, Article 4(2) of the European Convention for the Protection of Human Rights and Fundamental Freedoms, and the International Labour Office Convention for the Suppression of Forced or Compulsory Labour, both prohibit the imposition of compulsory unpaid work outside an institution. Thus a community service order without consent would contravene Britain's obligations under these Conventions. Secondly, there is a tiny minority of offenders who do refuse to consent to a community service order, usually by intimating this to the probation officer before the sentence. Since they would probably be uncooperative if a community service order were imposed against their wishes, they would be unlikely to complete their sentence satisfactorily. The requirement of consent thus bars some offenders who are unsuitable in any case. As the Home Secretary said in Parliament, work performed under direct coercion without even the pretence of consent, would, if done at all, be of a very poor standard. Thirdly, neither the probation service nor voluntary agencies would be likely to lend their willing support to a scheme which did not require the offender's explicit consent to an order.

The requirement of consent does not vitiate the right to appeal against the imposition of a community service order. The difference in this respect from a probation order derives from the fact that the latter, although amounting to a sentence under the Criminal Appeal Act 1968, is not deemed by virtue of s.13(1) of the Powers of Criminal Courts Act 1973 to flow from conviction for any purposes other than those of the proceedings in which the order is made. Thus no right of appeal lies against it unless there is no valid consent (*R.* v. *Tucker* (1974), 59 Cr. App. R.71). The community service order, on the other hand, is a sentence which follows a conviction and is therefore susceptible to appeal against sentence in the ordinary way. Nevertheless, the need for consent means that in practice an appeal against a community service order will be very rare. Thus there is little opportunity for higher courts to lay down a consistent policy on its use.

The availability of suitable work

The statutory requirements that the court consider a social enquiry report and be satisfied as to the availability of suitable work before passing a community service order gives the probation service unprecedented control over the type of offender who receives the sentence.

The influence of probation officers on sentencing via the social enquiry report is in any case a strong one. Following the reports of the Interdepartmental Committee on the Business of the Criminal Courts (the Streatfeild Report) in 1961 and the Departmental Committee on the Probation Service (the Morison Report) in 1962, the probation officer's role in this field was considerably expanded. The distinction drawn by those Committees between actual recommendations for sentence and expressions of opinion about the likely effect of a particular sentence on an offender appears now to be almost totally ignored.[3] Probation officers habitually make recommendations on all types of sentence, including custodial disposals, and clearly do so in the light of all relevant considerations, including risk, the public interest, and the nature of the offence.[4] Such recommendations may be couched in euphemistic terms—'a short period of brisk routine', for example, meaning a detention centre order. Nevertheless, the intention remains clear.

The expectations of the Streatfeild Committee and the Morison Committee that probation officers could limit themselves to expressions of opinion were, of course, always unrealistic. An attempt to relate 'needs' to penal measures must inevitably take account of the tariff or retributive perspective built into the penal system; the probation officer must consider the practicable options open to the court and try to reach a compromise within those options. The alternative is likely to be a totally unrealistic and even ludicrous recommendation.

Even sentencers are ambivalent on this question. In *R. v. Blowers*, [1977] Crim. L.R. 51, for example, Lawton L. J. criticized the probation officer for an unrealistic recommendation of a community service order in a case where the seriousness of the offence made imprisonment the only possible disposal. Conversely, in *R. v. Mulcahy* (no 4881/C/76)[5] Waller L. J. said:

> The social enquiry report recommended a Community Service Order or probation and the Judge criticized that recommendation. In that regard it is only fair to say that the probation officer's duty is to recommend what he or she thinks is most appropriate for the individual, without having regard necessarily to the public consequences, and although it is clearly an unrealistic approach in this particular case, Community

Service Orders are intended to take the place of imprisonment and should only be made where imprisonment would be appropriate in the first place.

Whatever the attitude of sentencers, the point remains that it is academic and artificial to draw a distinction between recommendations and expressions of opinion. Probation officers are not expected to usurp the judicial function, but they must nevertheless make recommendations which are realistic and do not jeopardize the court's confidence in their reports. Thus their recommendations, particularly at magistrates' court level, are likely to have a greater effect than they would if merely recognized as expressions of opinion about the likely effects of sentence.

Several studies have indicated that where social enquiry reports are prepared, a high proportion of them, especially in magistrates' courts, include clear and unambiguous recommendations. The proportion has ranged from 60 per cent to up to 93 per cent.[6] Similarly all studies have shown a high concordance between recommendations and sentences, usually between 70 per cent and 80 per cent.[7]

It is possible that the high concordance found between recommendation and sentence is a result of probation officers' tailoring their recommendations to conform to the policy of the court, and that sentencers would have chosen that sentence irrespective of the recommendation. For two reasons, however, this is unlikely to be so. First, the interaction between sentencers and probation officers probably conforms, in part, to what has been called 'the closed loop system of influence' (Davies, 1974), in which each side operates to confirm and support the expectations and practices of the other. Thus a probation officer's recommendation may well influence the decision of the court, but that decision will in turn influence the future recommendations that the officer makes. Secondly, there is some small evidence that magistrates do alter their decisions as a result of information and recommendations in social enquiry reports. In a study by Hood and Taylor (1968) magistrates were asked, when remanding an offender for a social enquiry report, to record an interim decision. Of the ninety-two social enquiry reports prepared, forty-four resulted in a change in the decision originally contemplated, although the magistrates were unable to specify the reasons for their change of mind. Davies also cited an unpublished study by Mott which provided 'further evidence of the extent to which magistrates appear to change their minds about the sentence after reading the social enquiry report' (Davies, 1974: p. 27).

The important and influential role which probation officers play in selecting the appropriate sentence thus cannot be doubted. The probation service, therefore, has a marked degree of control over the intake into any sentence which it is required to administer. When it comes to the selection of offenders for the community service order, this control intensifies. The requirements that the court consider a social enquiry report and be satisfied as to the availability of suitable work are both unusual in the sentencing of adult offenders.

The only parallel to the specific requirement for consideration of a social enquiry report in the case of an adult is contained in s.45 of the Powers of Criminal Courts Act 1973 (formerly s.57 of the Criminal Justice Act 1967), by which the Secretary of State is empowered to pass rules requiring a court to consider a social enquiry report before passing a particular type of sentence. This power has not yet been used. Instead the Home Secretary in 1968 addressed a circular (no. 188/1968) to all courts recommending that they should, as a normal practice, consider a social enquiry report on an offender aged 17 and over before passing:

1. a detention centre order;
2. a sentence of Borstal training;
3. a prison sentence of two years or less (including a suspended sentence) where the offender had not previously been subject to imprisonment (including a suspended sentence) or Borstal training;
4. a sentence of imprisonment on a woman.

The circular also drew attention to the view of the Morison Committee that a social enquiry report should normally be obtained before a probation order was imposed. A Home Office circular, of course, is not binding, and these recommendations are sometimes ignored.

The court is sometimes required to take into account certain information before passing a particular type of sentence. For example, s.20 of the Powers of Criminal Courts Act 1973 requires the court to take account of any information before them relevant to character or physical or mental condition before imposing a prison sentence on an offender on whom such a sentence has not previously been passed. But such a provision places no duty upon the court to obtain such information, whether by means of a social enquiry report or otherwise (*R*. v. *Ampleford* (1975), 62 Cr. App.R. 325). The statutory obligation to obtain a probation officer's report before imposing a community service order is therefore unprecedented in dealing with adults.

It is also plausible to suppose that sentencers will tend to rely heavily on the advice and recommendations of probation officers in the case of a new sentence which is unfamiliar to them. Apparently the Home Office envisaged that probation officers would be closely involved in the sentencing process, at least in the early stages of the scheme:

> If a report does not make a recommendation regarding community service, it is not expected that a court would make an order without seeking the views of the probation service—either by way of a further written report or orally. . . . Nor is it expected that a court would reject a probation officer's specific recommendation regarding community service without good reasons. (Home Office Circular no. 197/1974: para. 25)

In the light of this, it is not surprising that the Home Office Research Unit produced some evidence from the pilot areas which suggested that fluctuation in the rate of making community service orders was due more to changes in the number of probation officer recommendations than to changes in the number of court initiations (Pease *et al.*, 1975: p. 31).

In practice, the requirement that the court ascertain that suitable work is available also compels sentencers to rely heavily upon the probation service. Although courts have occasionally maintained that they can ascertain the availability of suitable work simply from their general knowledge of the scheme in the area, the more common interpretation of the legislation is that the community service organizer must confirm that a placement is available, either directly or via the probation officer preparing the social enquiry report. This virtually gives the organizer a power of veto over the making of an order. A few analogies to such a power exist. The Mental Health Act 1959 requires a recommendation by two doctors before a hospital order can be imposed, and under ss.3−4 of the Powers of Criminal Courts Act 1973 the court needs to be satisfied that arrangements have been made for treatment or attendance before imposing a probation order with a condition of psychiatric treatment or attendance at a day training centre.

It should be noted that there is no requirement that the probation officer should recommend a community service order; indeed, the courts can and do overrule negative recommendations. The power of veto lies in the fact that the availability of suitable work is partly determined by the nature of the offence and the character and circumstances of the offender. Thus an organizer can maintain that no suitable work could be found, for example, because the instability of the offender or the seriousness of his offence would present an unjustifiable risk to the community.

3

The philosophy

Broadly speaking, the three penal philosophies underlying the introduction of the community service order, as demonstrated in Chapter 1, were punishment, reparation, and reintegration. However, no attempt was made to analyse how these objectives might all be achieved within the single legislative and administrative framework of the community service order, nor the extent to which they might conflict. The fact that the sentence was firmly embedded in pragmatic politics precluded such an analysis. The endeavour to reconcile these often competing objectives has continued and taken the form of a debate about the use of the sentence as a tariff measure, determined by reference to the seriousness of the offence and incorporating elements of punishment and reparation, and its use as an individualized measure, chosen for its ability to meet the perceived needs of the offender.[1]

But how have these philosophies been elaborated and related to the community service order in practice, and how valid and relevant are they to the operation of the scheme? Upon what philosophical basis does the probation service administer the scheme, and what grounds are used for recommending the sentence? How much and for what reasons do probation areas differ in their practical implementation of the sentence? These questions were examined by reference to the practice of five different probation areas within England and Wales—Suffolk, Kent, Nottinghamshire, Bedfordshire, and Cambridgeshire.[2]

Empirical observation of the administration of community service schemes and of the way in which orders were implemented and their objectives perceived by the probation service in these areas took three main forms. First, each community service organizer was interviewed at length. A semi-structured questionnaire was used in order to ensure that all topics of possible concern were covered, while at the same time allowing the organizer some flexibility in describing the scheme from his or her own perspective. Informal discussions were also held with the organizer and members of staff on a number of occasions, and staff meetings were attended in Bedford and Nottingham. Secondly, social enquiry reports in six magistrates' courts in the areas concerned were studied in respect of a sample of offenders sentenced over a twelve-month period.[3] The courts chosen were Ipswich, Medway, Nottingham City, North Bedfordshire, Peterborough and Cambridge City.[4] Thirdly, files on offenders undergoing community service were examined to monitor their progress, and to discover the type of work performed, the number of unjustifiable absences from work, and the circumstances in which breach or revocation proceedings were contemplated or taken.

In discussing the penal philosophy of a sentence, a distinction must be drawn at the outset between the purposes for which a court imposes a sentence and the way in which that sentence is construed by the offender. It is often argued or assumed that any sentence that is experienced as unpleasant by an individual upon whom it is imposed must be described as punishment, whatever its stated objectives; that the definition of a punishment resides in the result, not the motive. This is to confuse the aims of a sentence with its functions. Punishment is something which is inflicted on an individual with the aim that it will be experienced as unpleasant. A sentence can have the aim of rehabilitating but also serve the function in some cases of punishing; or vice versa. That does not invalidate its description as a measure with a rehabilitative or punitive philosophy. It is only relevant—indeed, it only makes sense—to discuss the philosophical bases of a sentence in terms of the aims for which it is imposed.

Those aims, of course, might be unrealistic: the sentence might be ineffective or even counter-productive. Moreover, it might have consequences that were not thought of or intended. For example, community service organizers uniformly experience difficulty in predicting an offender's response to a community service order. For some it is a pleasant diversion from an otherwise boring life, a constructive outlet for their abilities and energies. In other cases it is a resented chore throughout, especially if it has supplanted activities that the offender enjoyed. For a third group, it begins as an unpleasant experience and finishes as an activity from which they derive a great deal of satisfaction. This diverse and fairly unpredictable response, however, does not affect the description of the philosophies underlying the use of the sentence; it merely bears upon the functions which it serves.

Punishment

Attempts to make the work punitive in itself have always been firmly resisted by those engaged in the administration of community service schemes. Any suggestion of hard labour or a chaingang concept would clearly be anathema to the probation service. In accordance with the original intention, therefore, the community service order has been implemented as a punishment only by the deprivation of leisure:

> The element of punishment in Community Service Orders derives from the loss of the offender's leisure time and not from the nature of the work itself. To introduce the element of punishment into the actual task would undermine the rehabilitative aims of the scheme. To borrow a comment once made about prisons, Community Service Orders are imposed as punishment, but not *for* punishment. (Nottinghamshire Probation and After-care Service, 1975: p. 15)

Courts, of course, have sometimes expressed the hope that the work will not be too soft, and have occasionally gone so far as to suggest what type of work the offender should be engaged in. Community service organizers, too, especially in areas with schemes just commencing (Ipswich, for example) have sometimes indicated what the work placement might involve. However, it has always been understood that the legislation does not permit the court to specify what type of work should be performed under a community service order: that must be left to the discretion of the individual organizer. An indication to the court of a likely placement, therefore, is not in any sense treated as binding, and it is without doubt that the choice of work is not governed by penal considerations. Isolated examples of work directly related to the nature of the offence can be found. For instance, it was reported that 'the punishment is fitting the crime at the Ironbridge Gorge in Shropshire', when an offender convicted of various motoring offences was given a very slow dumper truck to drive (*The Times*, 19/2/73). These, however, have been coincidental rather than deliberate.

The power of the deprivation of leisure to effect punishment should not be underrated. As Radzinowicz and King have pointed out:

> Leisure is still a highly valued commodity, a time for freedom. As an alternative to the complete deprivation of freedom implicit in imprisonment, the partial deprivation of leisure seems a good compromise. (Radzinowicz and King, 1977: p. 302)

Moreover, the community service order imposes strict demands upon the offender to attend for work as and when he is instructed to do so; failure to meet these demands can result in a fine or a sentence for the original offence. It is not easy, especially in conjunction with full-time employment, to complete an order approaching the maximum of 240 hours within the stipulated twelve months. It may require considerable self-discipline and is certainly an obligation which many do not relish. There is a world of difference between doing community service work because one wants to and doing it because one is forced to.

Reparation

The idea that reparation should be required of offenders has not been discarded, although it has had little direct influence on the way in which orders have been implemented. The theme was apparent in many social enquiry reports studied here, for example:

> In many ways he appears to be a responsible young man and I think should be required to make some reparation to others for the offences.

> Community service could provide opportunities for Mr S to make some tangible reparation to the community.

> The court may feel that perhaps community service is an appropriate way to deal with this man, where he can return to the community payment for his continual offending against it.

This reparative element of the community service order is alleged to fulfil a general obligation to recompense society which, as an abstract entity, has been notionally injured. By performing work of benefit to the community, the offender is converted from being a drain on its resources to being a useful contributor to its general welfare—thus somehow 'repairing' the damage he has caused.

However, this is a nebulous philosophy, deriving from a confused attempt to extend the concept of personal reparation beyond the limits within which it has any sensible application. As Mr Silkin suggested in Parliament, it is one thing for an offender to make reparation to an old lady from whom he has stolen money; it is quite a different matter to clean a canal or work in a home for the mentally handicapped in order to reimburse society in general (H.C. Debates, Standing Committee G, 10/2/72: cols 522–3). Indeed, the latter, which may be called 'symbolic reparation', is closely allied to some versions of retributivism as a justification for punishment. It has overtones of the Hegelian notion that retribution is the annulment or cancellation of the wrongful act.[5] It is also closely allied to Kneale's doctrine of 'moral accounting'. He pointed out that the language of punishment is closely related to notions of payments, debts and duties, and went on to say:

> Sometimes, by a further extension of the commercial analogy, punishment is considered as a negative wage earned by wrongdoing. . . . When we talk of punishment as retribution we have a similar conception in mind. In this case payment is supposed to be made by the punishing authority, but it is payment of something undesirable, i.e., what I have called a negative wage, and the purpose of the payment is to settle the wrongdoer's moral account. (Kneale, 1967: p. 177)

According to this theory, then, retribution is the process by which the offender *is paid back* by society for his wrongdoing. Symbolic reparation through the community service order, on the other hand, is commonly alleged to be the process by which the offender *pays back* society for his offending. However, this is an artificial distinction. Both have the underlying motive of the restoration of balance to the social order. Payment by the offender to society, as distinct from its individual members, can sensibly be understood only as a means of cancelling out the offence in a retributive sense. It is true that retribution is commonly understood to be the repayment of an evil with an evil, whereas community service is designed to benefit society. But the fact that the payment takes the form of work that will help some person or persons in need does not of itself make reparation an apt description of it. It might merely make it a more appropriate retributive sentence than, say, imprisonment, which often works to the disadvantage of both society and the offender. No doubt reparation has a certain public appeal, since it imposes obligations upon the criminal, rather than his simply being a burden upon society. It is also more fashionable than a retributive philosophy. Nevertheless, it is difficult to avoid the conclusion that it is simply a euphemism, albeit a politic one, for elements which have previously been embodied in some versions of retributivism.

Expiation

A further perspective has also been injected into the reparative idea since the inception of community service schemes, with the view, succinctly stated by the Bedford community service organizer, that it can serve as a channel for the need some offenders feel 'to make some tangible amends for their irreponsible behaviour'. Proponents of this view argue that community service is a useful device for some offenders with strong guilt feelings, which can be assuaged by the performance of useful work for others. Winfield, the Durham community service organizer, for example, claimed:

> Many offenders express the need, either consciously or otherwise, to pay —if not exactly in kind—for what they have done. Probation officers seem to recognize the importance of this emotional need and the concluding paragraphs of many S.I.R.s containing recommendations for community service state that 'the imposition of a Community Service Order will be a constructive means of the defendant repaying his debt to society'. (Winfield, 1977: p. 127)

It is a misnomer to describe this as reparation, as that implies a payment for the benefit of others. A more appropriate representation of the intention behind it is provided by the notion of expiation or atonement: the process by which an offender can absolve his guilt.

The need for expiation is thought to derive not only from the commission of the offence in question, but from the accumulation of failures which so often characterizes an offender's past life. The Nottingham community service organizer stated:

> The reparative element in community service can help an offender to shed a burden of guilt; not only the obvious guilt deriving from some damage he may clearly have inflicted upon others by an offence, but the often inexplicable or disproportionate guilt derived from some forgotten action or omission, or even some imaginary sin. Certainly this kind of compulsive guilt is often suspected in some cases of compulsive offending, but the impossibility of bringing the cause of the guilt to conscious awareness makes its absolution difficult. It may be that among the Community Service successes already documented there are some which, quite unknown to us, fall into this category. (Nottinghamshire Probation and After-care Service, 1975: pp. 5–6)

This sentiment is practically indistinguishable from a major aspect of the rehabilitative philosophy of the community service order, which holds that by the enhancement of self-esteem and the overcoming of feelings of inferiority the offender can attain a legitimate status in society.

Rehabilitation

While punitive and reparative components in the sentence have not been ignored, most attention has been paid by community service organizers and other probation officers to the objective of rehabilitation. The general importance of community involvement has remained a central theme. Winfield has argued that the community service order embodies 'the maxim of work *with* the community as opposed to work *for* the community' (Winfield, 1977: p. 128). Of course, this idea of a partnership between the offender and the community has sprung from the aspirations of the reintegrative perspective discussed earlier. It has now been refined and supplemented by a number of specific hypotheses about the rehabilitative potential of the community service order. Broadly, it is believed that the community service order may rehabilitate through any of the following: the fostering of social responsibility; contact with other workers; the constructive use of leisure time; the development of long-term interests and skills, and even new employment prospects (termed 'New Careers'); and the resumption of a work habit by the unemployed and unemployable.

a. The fostering of social responsibility
When the community service order was introduced, importance was attached to the performance of work for individual beneficiaries, so that offenders could come into personal contact with those in need. The implication was that contact with the elderly, deprived and disabled—people often worse off than themselves—would instil into offenders a sense of social responsibility and give them a new outlook on their role in society. This hope has remained central to the claim that community service can serve a rehabilitative function. The means by which social responsibility might be encouraged have not only been made more specific but have also been given a broader basis.

First, the suggestion, when the community service legislation was discussed in Parliament, that many offenders—particularly the young—were egocentric, has found some support. The Durham community service organizer said of the young adult offender:

> He is capable of the extremes of utter selfishness at one time and of self-sacrifice, devotion and loyalty at another. (Durham Probation and After-care Service, 1975: p. 14)

It is argued that the appeal to his ideals and loyalty might counteract the other side of his personality—his self-centred preoccupation; by helping those in need, he might develop a sense of community involvement and commitment to others. In Nottingham a social enquiry report stated:

> Although at present Mr X's life looks promising, his attitudes would appear to be very self-centred. The Court might therefore consider that a period of usefully giving to others would benefit this man.

Secondly, and more importantly, it is postulated that by creating a situation in which an offender can make a positive contribution to community needs and thereby experience achievement, he will develop an improved self-image and a greater realization of his value as an individual in society. The concentration upon the positive aspects of his character, and the utilization of his talents and skills, might render his negative attributes and antisocial tendencies less important in his over-all social functioning. This in turn might give him a more social and responsive outlook towards others, and thereby reduce the risk of reoffending. This was the basis of recommendations in many social enquiry reports in the courts studied here, for example:

> A community service order will offer him the satisfaction and opportunity of being a contributing member of the community, which he does not feel at the present time and which will be an essential factor in his rehabilitation.

> I feel he has attributes which he could usefully offer for the benefit of others and would regain self-respect by doing so.

> I feel that this action (a community service order) could assist Mr X to discover for himself a feeling of worth and thereby enable him to take his place as a useful citizen in the community.

> A community service order could help him to increase his confidence and self-image and do more to achieve his potential in life.

The language in which such recommendations were couched was often strikingly similar. Self-respect, self-worth, self-esteem, self-confidence, improved self-image: these recurred time and again. The central feature of this view is that the community service order provides an opportunity for the offender to find 'an alternative and legitimate source of achievement and status' (West, 1976: p. 74). The sentence, therefore, has remained explicitly reintegrative in intention: it is a way of creating an outlet for undeveloped potential and unrecognized ability and skills among those who have been regarded as failures and outcasts.

It is important to note three distinctions between this mode of rehabilitation and that attempted under the probation order. First, the traditional approach of the probation service, based essentially upon social casework principles (however they are for the time being defined), has been preoccupied with the offender's shortcomings and failures. Thus it has concentrated upon devising solutions to those problems which have been viewed as the root cause of his offending. The community service order, on the other hand, is concerned with utilizing the positive attributes of the offender. In essence, it is an ability-oriented rather than a problem-oriented approach. Offenders performing community service thus become the dispensers rather than the recipients of material and personal aid. Paradoxically, this simultaneously perpetuates a rehabilitative ideology and turns it on its head: offenders become both helpers and the focus of help. Secondly, while the requirements of the probation order are normally fulfilled within the sanctuary of the office or home interview, work under the community service order is usually performed in full view of the outside community. Thus the offender must behave in a responsible and socially acceptable manner. Although the community service organizer may still allow considerable latitude according to individual circumstances, the sentence in principle treats the offender as responsible and holds him accountable to the community for his actions, instead of shielding him from it. Thirdly, the community service order has a fixed and limited content directed towards the fulfilment of a clearly defined objective ordered by the court. This sets out the nature and limits of the obligations of both offender and organizer. The offender's obligations to perform a fixed number of hours' work has its corollary in the organizer's obligation to provide the necessary work placements and the supervision and equipment to enable the work to be done. The fixed work content also provides an identifiable measurement of the order's successful completion. This is all in stark contrast to the vague, diffuse, and often global objectives of the probation order.[6]

These theoretical distinctions are not without some practical significance. Whether rehabilitation is accomplished or not, the sentence provides offenders with an experience which they can readily understand and respond to: it is thus a welcome departure from the problem-oriented approach of the probation order. For instance, in a survey of 100 offenders who successfully completed community service orders in Nottingham between 1973 and 1975,[7] it was found that these particular offenders almost unanimously preferred the experience of the community service order to that of the probation order (although fourteen had not had probation as such and the rest had by definition 'failed' on probation, at least in terms of recidivism). Probation was usually described as a process of aimless talk. Their feelings about community service, on the other hand, were summarized as follows:

> . . . the positive aspects of CS, as seen by these men and women, were its variety, its flexibility, its direct practical application in many instances, its offering acceptance, trust, opportunity. The importance of its *boundaries* came out time and again, especially when compared with the rather amorphous experience of Probation, reporting over what seemed like life-long periods. In this respect numbers of hours, and working at jobs, made sense. (Flegg *et al.*, 1976: p. 24)

However, it has been insufficiently recognized that the offender's reintegration into the community depends on a change not only in the offender's social attitudes, but also in the attitudes of the community towards the offender. In other words, the offender's image of himself and society's image of him must begin to converge, so that the effects of stigmatization and alienation are neutralized. If this is a practicable objective, it is likely to be a gradual process, with only a limited impact on mass opinion. There has generally been no lack of support for the scheme, particularly from voluntary organizations. However, community attitudes are hard to change: beneficiaries or voluntary organizations who were wary of offenders at the outset tend to remain so after one or even several successful placements, refusing to generalize from good experiences with individual offenders. Conversely, those who accept offenders unquestioningly are the ones who do not stigmatize them in any case.

A more fundamental criticism which can be levelled at the reintegrative perspective in community service, at least given its present depth of analysis, is the absence of any comprehensive discussion or questioning of the concept of 'community'. In defining the needs that community service workers should attempt to meet, a largely consensual view of society has been accepted. It appears to have been assumed that the interests of one group are compatible with the interests of others in the community. Hence the ideology of *service* for the community rather than simply work within it.

This is essentially an idealistic vision of society. 'Community' is not a unitary concept, and the interests of one group do sometimes clash with those of another. Recent years bear witness to this; those involved in community work have increasingly called into question the effectiveness of consensual styles of social change, and of the orthodox image of voluntary service. Thus community involvement has sometimes embraced elements of radicalism and has emphasized control by the working classes over their own destiny. In the process of exercising such control (which, of course, the expansion of voluntary service was trying to encourage), these consumers have sometimes been prepared to take direct action which has placed them on the fringe of or beyond legality. This is manifested in the development of groups such as tenants' associations, claimants' unions, and squatters' groups.

Thus voluntary service, instead of projecting a middle-class image, is increasingly questioning the values, power structures, and distribution of resources in modern society. The helpers and the helped are encouraged to work in partnership, to work for change and to work towards the development of independence and community self-help. The implications of this new image of voluntary service have never been properly explored in the context of the community service order.

First, who is to define the needs of the community? If the community service order is to foster a sense of social responsibility by enabling the offender to make a personal contribution to the meeting of community needs, then the offender himself must surely see the work in that light. This was recognized by Mr Silkin in the parliamentary debates on the 1972 Criminal Justice Bill, when he stated:

> If it is intended that this [the community service scheme] will operate through any voluntary agency which has a concern with the needs of the community, irrespective of its own individual philosophy and objectives, clearly that raises wide questions about the kind of work which one ought to compel an offender to perform. . . . The Bill recognizes that there are difficulties over this question by making provision for objection on religious grounds. (H.C. Debates, Standing Committee G, 8/2/72: col. 450)

In reply, however, the Under-Secretary of State pointed out that it would be possible for the offender to object on religious grounds only to the time, not the type, of work. In other words, the definition of relevant community needs was left entirely to the discretion of the individual community service organizer. When the experimental community service schemes first commenced, Radical Alternatives to Prison (RAP) attacked the concept underlying the Inner London scheme on the basis that it reflected a middle-class ideology:

> Any allocated task is likely to reflect middle-class objectives and values, possibly illustrated by the present preoccupation with environmental problems. Such tasks are unlikely to commend themselves to the working-class offender who is likely to see more immediate personal and social problems as having priority. Without the tailoring of the projects to needs that the offender identifies as important, there is an obvious likelihood of rejection. When faced with menial labour and deprived of his leisure time, the chances that an individual will 'learn to appreciate the needs of others' are very slim indeed. (Uglow, 1973: p. 3)

As RAP later admitted (Uglow, 1975), this criticism was overstated, as most of the work imposed under community service has been imaginative and directed towards generally recognized needs. The handicapped, for instance, are likely to be viewed as generally deserving of help by all sections of the community. Moreover, at least in some areas, work has been chosen to accord with the offender's own view of what constitutes 'need'. The Nottingham community service organizer stated that in her area community service was explained to an offender as a service to an individual or group which the offender himself personally regarded as deserving of help, and that an explanation on these terms would usually elicit a positive response from the offender (Nottinghamshire Probation and After-care Service, 1975: p. 13).

Nevertheless, RAP's initial cynicism was not entirely misplaced. Practical constraints upon the choice of work in areas with smaller caseloads and a less established network of voluntary organizations may make the link with needs in the offender's own community fairly tenuous on occasions. For example, what about canal clearance; archaeological digs; the clearance of a cemetery; the construction of a maritime museum; the digging of foundations for a new wall at a local church; or work for a local railway society? Mere social or geographical proximity of the task to the offender's own community environment does not provide a guarantee of the personal or social relevance of the work experience. Unless it is relevant, though, the offender is unlikely to appreciate the value of his contribution; instead, community service schemes may merely 'provide a means for channelling deviants into socially approved pursuits which might do little to enable the offender to interpret or analyse his own or her own anti-social experiences, and thus do not stimulate any real movement' (Swain, 1975: p. 34).

A related issue is the ethical dilemma in which the community service organizer might be placed when the interests of different community groups conflict. Should offenders be placed only with orthodox voluntary and statutory organizations, meeting conventionally defined needs in conventional ways, or should they also be placed with some less socially acceptable groups, whose concerns might have more immediate relevance to the offender's own definition of 'community needs'? The Durham community service organizer, recognizing this problem, stated:

> It would be a sad day indeed if the Probation Service were to discriminate between contentious and non-contentious projects, choosing the latter for the sake of, say, inter-departmental relationships. We should not deny our clients the opportunity of working with community groups —e.g. tenants associations—simply because such groups, on occasions, 'rock the boat' with the authorities. (Durham Probation and After-care Service, 1975: p. 15)

However, in general this is an issue that has not been confronted; the uncritical acceptance of conventional definitions of 'needs' tends to exclude those groups who actively challenge the *status quo*.

b. Contact with other workers

The importance of the wholesome influence of other non-offender volunteers was stressed when the community service order was introduced. However, this is now a minor consideration; specific mention of it was made in only one social enquiry report examined here. The hope that offenders would take over the altruism and moral conscience which volunteers were presumed to possess was always rather unrealistic; mere contact with others does not seem to be enough to change attitudes in other situations, and there is no reason why it should be in the work context. Nevertheless, importance is still attached to the value of work alongside others (whether voluntary workers, supervisors, or other offenders) for three reasons.

First, it is seen as an opportunity for offenders, especially through the medium of group work, not to take over the values of others, but to form their own positive social values. Groups 'may develop a microcosmic concept of community, and the element of concern for others'. They may therefore be 'appropriately critical or supportive' and enable each other 'to achieve a more generally acceptable level of functioning' (Nottinghamshire Probation and After-care Service, 1975: p. 5). This view was well illustrated by one social enquiry report in Nottingham:

> Mr X could be accommodated in a community service work group, where he would not only have the benefit of helping the community but he himself would receive benefit by way of group interaction and discipline.

Secondly, work with a suitable supervisor who, as an authority figure, can teach the offender to adopt a more realistic attitude towards his social and employment obligations, is often seen as the key to successful community service for some offenders. In particular, it is perceived as a way of breaking down anti-authority attitudes, and encouraging adherence to the reasonable demands which society places upon its members. This implication, for example, was contained in two other social enquiry reports in Nottingham:

> This [a practical work group] would appear to be a good setting in which to tackle the problems presented, such as his anti-authority attitude . . . and to provide a counter-balance to his present peer group.

> He may develop a more positive relationship with an authority figure in the more informal work setting.

The supervisor is also expected to play an essential part in shaping the offender's over-all reaction to the work experience. In particular,

he may be able to interpret the value of the work for the offender—
perhaps by pointing out that toys being made or mended in a workshop are for children without fathers.

Thirdly, it is believed that working alongside others may help to
combat social isolation and enable an offender to become more
adept at forming relationships with other workers and supervisors.
The skills thus learned may be applied to relationships in other
social or employment situations, so that the offender is able to cope
more satisfactorily with the demands and conflicts of everyday life.

c. The constructive use of leisure time

Another feature of the community service order that has received
increasing attention, especially since the scheme was extended
nationally, is its constructive occupation of leisure time among
those who might otherwise expend their energies in antisocial ways.
This has been presented as the primary reason for some recommendations for community service, for example:

> Since X's drug-taking activities have been confined to week-ends, I have
> discussed with him the possibility of occupying some of this time under a
> community service order. X would see this as constructive.

> X is a robust and healthy young man with, it seems, a good deal of
> excess energy and time on his hands, which could be better spent in more
> constructive pursuits.

There are two facets of this.

In the first instance, work during leisure time might reduce the
opportunity to commit crime. Hence the popular belief that it is
appropriate for football hooligans, in order to prevent them from
attending football matches. This is not so much rehabilitative as
incapacitative, and it has occasionally found practical expression in
work instructions. In one case in Ipswich, for instance, the
organizer instructed an offender with several previous convictions
for violence at Ipswich Town Football Club to work on Saturdays
at Felixstowe. *Inter alia*, he was placed at Felixstowe, some distance
from Ipswich, in order to prevent his absconding to attend a match.
There is also an informal agreement between the probation service
and the magistracy in one area that if football hooligans are recommended for community service by probation officers, they will
frequently be given it on the understanding that they are instructed
to do the work on Saturday afternoons.

However, field probation officers have usually rejected this
degree of specificity in making recommendations for community
service, as theirs is not the task of deciding when and where the
work is to be done. Instead, they have relied upon the idea that

constructive occupation of leisure time will reduce the *motivation* to commit crime. It is believed that offending is often the result of boredom and aimlessness, especially among the young; thus community service, in usefully occupying their free time and providing a creative outlet for their energies and abilities, might obviate the need to participate in less desirable activities. Again, this depends upon the view that concentration upon positive abilities can counteract antisocial traits and prevent their manifestation.

d. 'New Careers'

The most optimistic hope for the community service order has been that the offender might identify and develop talents and interests of which he had not previously been aware, and that he might therefore become a more permanent community resource by continuing as a voluntary worker after the end of the order, or perhaps even by the formation of new employment aspirations. This theme was evident in a number of social enquiry reports:

> I feel that X is likely to continue with voluntary service if he once becomes established.

> It [a community service order] is thought to be an appropriate sentence in view of her expressed interest in a future career in one of the caring professions such as residential work with children, the disabled, or elderly.

> He wonders if his experience of community service might ultimately lead to a change of employment for him.

Such statements have parallels in other attempts to train and use former and potential 'clients' as employees of social welfare agencies, which have collectively become known as the 'New Careers' movement. It began with the anti-poverty programmes of the United States in the 1960s when hundreds of people from socially disadvantaged groups were employed to operate within their own communities, in order to bridge the apparently wide gulf between professionals and their clients. Its influence was felt in Britain by the early 1970s, and has resulted in a number of small schemes— including the use of a hostel at Bristol to train young offenders as social workers.

There have been isolated examples of offenders taking up full-time jobs with an organization after their placement there under a community service order, but this is a rare occurrence. Slightly more common is the discovery or development of an interest or talent which the offender can utilize in an employment situation and thus improve his job prospects; but this too can easily be exaggerated. Indeed, there is a danger that by providing the offender with an alternative set of values, skills, expectations, and patterns of behaviour in the work context, the community service scheme will give an unrealistic hope of more fulfilling job opportunities which will not in practice be available to him. A more realistic hope is that the offender will continue as a voluntary worker, so that the transitory benefits of the community service order, both to the offender and to the community, will become more permanent.

The importance of this to the over-all rehabilitative strategy of the community service order should not be overstated. It is true that the continuation of offenders in voluntary work is a widely publicized feature of many schemes. The Nottinghamshire community service organizer reported during the experimental period that 'over 40 per cent of those interviewed on completion of community service expressed commitment to continue involvement on a voluntary basis' (Harding, 1974: p. 481). Moreover, it is an integral feature of most reports of the 'success stories' of community service (e.g. Seavers and Collins, 1977). However, it has never been regarded as a *sine qua non* of the rehabilitative process; rather, it is merely a way of providing the offender with continuing opportunities to experience legitimate achievement and success if he should want them. Organizers do not expect the majority of offenders to continue community service work voluntarily; and those offenders who do usually pursue it for only a short time (see, for example, Nottinghamshire Probation and After-care Service, 1975: pp. 32–3).

e. The resumption of a work habit
At the commencement of the experimental community service schemes, one of the criteria for selection for the community service order was the existence of a reasonable work record.[8] However, it has since been found that an individual's work record is a very poor indicator of his response to community service, as some long-term unemployed perform well. The existence of an erratic employment history, therefore, is no longer treated as *prima facie* evidence that an order is unsuitable. Instead, it is believed that community service can be used as a device to help the chronically unemployed to re-establish a work habit, although it is recognized that such offenders must be chosen with care and that limited success only may be achieved (Durham Probation and After-care Service, 1975: p. 30; Nottinghamshire Probation and After-care Service, 1975: p. 6). In a few social enquiry reports this was mentioned as a major objective:

[Of a woman who had not worked for over three years.] Community service should be considered so that she establishes a work pattern while receiving a high degree of support under a probation order [to which she was already subject].

[Of a man unemployed for the last eighteen months.] The objective [of the community service order] would be to help in restoring X's self-confidence and assist him in testing out his capacity to actually do a job of work.

A community service order does offer potentially the opportunity to X of some satisfying work experiences which may well improve his motivation to pursue appropriate full-time employment.

The court will be aware that X has not earned his living for some years and possibly a community service order would introduce this idea into his mind as a workable proposition for the future.

For such offenders, community service is in effect regarded as a sheltered work situation whereby they can be gradually eased back into a work routine. This is based upon the premise that people who are unemployed or viewed as unemployable can develop self-confidence and good work habits if they are placed in work situations where allowance is made, at least initially, for their employment difficulties.

The perceived relevance of the development of a work habit to the prevention of crime is twofold. First, it derives from the strongly held belief that idleness encourages criminality. In Inner London, for example, it has recently been stated that 'for a large number of probationers and ex-prisoners being supervised, the prospect of rehabilitation and a lawful productive life are considerably diminished by chronic unemployment' (Inner London Probation and After-care Service, 1976: p. 61).

The use of work as a reformative device has been a recurrent theme for a long time, particularly inside institutions. As early as 1547, the so-called 'slavery statute' stated that idleness was 'the mother and root of all theft, robberies, and other evil acts and mischiefs'.[9] Hence the Houses of Correction, set up later in the century for idle vagabonds, included work for reformative rather than punitive purposes as an essential part of their regimes. The sentiment that industrious habits were essential to personal reformation was reiterated during the nineteenth century, the first half in particular. In 1838, for instance, the Third Report of the Inspectors of Prisons for the Home District stated:

The next quality which we deem indispensable to a sound system of prison discipline is the capacity of producing in the prisoner permanent

habits of useful labour. . . . Now, next to the inculcation of religious
duties, and to the preservation of character . . . nothing affords better
security for his good behaviour than the resources which habits of
industry confer.

It has also become a major theme in relation to the use of work
within prisons and Borstals in the twentieth century (see, for
example, Home Office, 1961: paras 20–30; Home Office, 1962:
paras 12–14).

Outside institutions, the requirement to 'lead an industrious life'
has been a regular condition of the probation order, and it has been
seen as part of the probation officer's function to help the offender
find employment. More recently, this has been extended by the
establishment of sheltered workshops for probationers and others,
and 'job creation' schemes such as the 'Bulldog' Employment
Project in Inner London.[10]

The second link that is thought to exist between the development
of a work habit and rehabilitation is grounded in the idea that the
ability to pay one's own way—to hold down a job—is an essential
part of the development of self-confidence and an improved self-
image which itself forms the basis of a sense of social responsibility. As West, the Nottingham community service organizer, put
it:

> Work is a measure of the value placed upon an individual in society. To
> be unemployed is to be valueless, to be underemployed is to be under-
> valued. (West, 1976: p. 83)

According to this view, work as a measure of personal value is not
purely a middle-class conception. It is a universal need and a
universal obligation: an essential component in the retention or
retrieval of self-respect.

*   *   *

It is apparent that the range of objectives that the community
service order was originally designed to achieve has not only been
retained but has been enlarged by the addition of a number of
different theories about its rehabilitative power. Although these
theories have been rendered fairly specific, they have nevertheless
extended rather than restricted the types of offenders to which the
sentence might be thought applicable. They have therefore
increased the potential for ambiguity and conflict in the way in
which the sentence is both used and implemented.

4

Administration and practice

The establishment of schemes

Prior to the availability of the community service order in a particular probation area, the practice from the outset was to appoint a community service organizer several months in advance in order to set up the administration necessary to implement orders. The normal period for which a community service organizer was appointed full time before community service orders became available to any courts in the area was about six months. During that time, his duties were fourfold.

His first and most important task was to establish contact with statutory and voluntary service organizations in the area, to select particular areas of need which could be met by work under a community service order, and to arrange for the availability of work placements with particular organizations. Resistance from local organizations had to be overcome or bypassed and a sufficient reservoir of work had to be developed to cater for the most optimistic estimate of the flow of offenders through the scheme. Often the initial job was to obtain agreement in principle to the scheme from co-ordinating bodies such as the local Council for Voluntary Service or the Social Services Committee of the local council, before particular work placements could be arranged. The nature of this task varied from area to area, depending on the co-operation received from local organizations and their willingness to participate in the scheme. The aim in all areas, of course, was to ensure that when the first community service orders were made by the courts, there would be a fairly wide range of work available.

Secondly, he had to undertake a more general public relations role and inform the community at large of the purpose of the scheme and its potential. This included talks to community groups, whether or not they might become participants in the scheme, as well as more general publicity.

The third task to be undertaken before community service orders

became available was to do as much as possible to inform probation officers and sentencers of the purpose of the order and the way
in which it would probably operate in that area. Meetings were held
with magistrates and judges, booklets were sometimes written for
use by probation officers, and circulars were distributed suggesting
certain criteria of eligibility for the sentence. Informal agreements
were also reached with local sentencers on the circumstances in
which it might be appropriate to use the order. In addition, organizers, to a greater or lesser extent, tried to involve field probation
officers in the initial planning. In Bedford, for example, a community service development group was set up with representatives
from all the probation offices in the area, so that they could participate in decisions on the development of the sentence and also
channel information back to other probation officers. Procedures
were devised for assessing offenders' suitability for community
service and standard forms were circulated to probation officers
for completion when offenders were being considered for the
sentence.

Once the sentence became available, of course, these tasks
obviously ceased to occupy the same amount of time. None the
less, they remained an important part of the organizer's job: good
public relations and adequate liaison with other probation officers
and the courts were necessary so that they were aware of the type of
work being performed. This was essential if the scheme was to be a
success and continue to be used by the courts.

The fourth task of the organizer was the appointment of the
administrative and secretarial staff necessary for the implementation of community service orders. In all five areas in this study,
organizers were senior probation officers. They all had their own
sets of offices and their own secretarial staff. Their assistants were
either trained probation officers seconded full time to the community service scheme, or ancillaries (called community service asso-
ciates or project officers) specially employed for the purpose. The
Home Office has tried to encourage schemes based mainly on
untrained ancillaries, but some areas, notably Nottingham, have
resisted this, believing that the administration of community
service requires experience and skill in dealing with offenders.

At the outset in each area, the community service team was
largely autonomous and independent of other probation work.
This situation, however, has been modified in some places by the
devolution of responsibility for the administration of community
service schemes to local probation offices. Varying degrees of
decentralization have taken place. Each of the probation areas
studied here has allowed partial devolution somewhere in the

county, by stationing the probation officers or ancillaries responsible for community service in local probation offices. While retaining their status as personnel solely engaged in community service administration and remaining under the direct control of the community service organizer in the county, they nevertheless have a closer working relationship with other probation officers than those who have remained within a separate community service unit. In Cambridgeshire, for example, the community service organizer's office is in Huntingdon, while the project officers responsible for the offenders residing in the Peterborough and Cambridge areas work from the local probation office in each city.

A more extreme form of devolution has taken place in Tunbridge Wells, Kent, and (apart from Greater Nottingham itself) in the whole of Nottinghamshire, whereby responsibility for the scheme is completely handed over to the local probation team. One or more officers within that team organizes the community service scheme in that area, while retaining a reduced caseload of probation and other statutory supervision orders. Over-all responsibility lies with the senior probation officer in charge of that team. The community service organizer for the county acts only as consultant and co-ordinator in such matters as the supply of tools and other equipment. In Tunbridge Wells, in fact, all formal links with the Kent community service organizer in Gillingham have been severed. To some extent this development has been prompted by the extension of community service schemes to small rural communities, where numbers are too small to warrant the employment of a full-time specialist community service officer. Organization by a specialist officer from another area appears to reduce the rapport with courts, probation officers and community organizations alike, and hence to hinder the scheme's growth. Delegation to a local probation officer has therefore been thought to provide the best solution. Moreover, it is believed that direct involvement by area officers in the scheme gives them a much greater awareness of community resources and community needs, and thus exercises a healthy influence on the rest of their work.

The possible effect of this development on the use of the sentence cannot be overlooked. As the autonomy of the community service team is increasingly broken down, and more and more field probation officers become involved in implementing orders, the variations in approach to the sentence and the ambiguity arising as a result, will inevitably increase. To that extent it is a development which must be viewed with some unease.

The procedure for assessing offenders' suitability for community service

Consideration of community service can be initiated by either the court or a probation officer preparing a social enquiry report on an offender. In the six courts studied here, it was clear that (at least in the early stages of the scheme) sentencers tended to depend heavily upon the probation service to determine which offenders were suitable for community service. In 200 out of 281 offenders receiving a community service order, the initial suggestion came from a probation officer.[1] In another fifty-two cases the orders were positively recommended by the probation officer or community service organizer following a suggestion from the court. In only seven cases was the probation officer or organizer definitely opposed to community service, and in five of these a work placement was nevertheless reluctantly made available. The court went ahead regardless and made orders in the other two cases as well. In each of these instances the organizer implemented the order, although it is arguable that he could have applied to the court immediately for its revocation in the interests of justice, on the grounds that the offender was unsuitable for any available work.

In this respect, as in others, variations between the courts were evident. A greater proportion of the orders in Peterborough were initiated by probation officers than in any other court: twenty-seven out of thirty-two. In contrast, the two courts in the pilot areas—Nottingham and Medway—whose schemes had been established three years earlier at the beginning of 1973, were clearly more independent of probation officers' advice. In Nottingham, 49 out of 162 orders were initiated by the court, and in Medway over one-fifth of the fifty-eight orders were made without a clear recommendation from a probation officer. This, of course, was only to be expected as courts gained more confidence in, and knowledge of, the sentence. Nevertheless, their use of the sentence was still no doubt influenced by the types of cases in which it had previously been recommended, and few negative recommendations were ignored.

The courts, of course, did not automatically follow recommendations in favour of community service. Only Bedford had no cases where a positive recommendation by a probation officer was rejected. In Nottingham there were thirty-six such cases, in Medway nine, in Ipswich six, and in Peterborough and Cambridge four. During the experimental period, too, the Home Office Research Unit found that the proportion of recommendations by probation officers for community service that were accepted varied from a very high 92 per cent in Inner London to only 48 per cent in Shropshire (Pease *et al.*, 1975: p. 24). Thus it may be concluded that courts are rather more willing to depart from positive than negative recommendations. Over-all, though, the strong influence of the probation service in determining the types of offenders who receive a community service order is undesirable.

Whether consideration of community service was initiated by the court or the probation officer preparing the social enquiry report, all five areas studied here followed the common practice of requiring referral to the community service team for confirmation of the availability of a work placement. In all areas except Medway this was done either at the time of the preparation of the social enquiry report or after an adjournment for the purpose, usually for three weeks. In Medway, stand-down enquiries were permitted; that is, the case could be put back until later in the same day while enquiries were made with the community service team—usually by the probation officer on court duty. This practice was strongly discouraged in the other areas, because it was felt that it did not allow time for proper consultation and assessment and encouraged the court to make orders without seeking proper advice in doubtful cases. For example, one of the offenders receiving a community service order in the Medway court was not enthusiastic about this sentence, and on a stand-down enquiry a probation officer in the community service team decided that an adjournment was needed so that he could be interviewed. Nevertheless, the court went ahead and made the order on the same day. On the other hand, stand-down enquiries obviated the need for further adjournments and thus encouraged a wider use of the sentence. For example, during the experimental period in Durham when the flow of orders was very irregular, the policy of allowing stand-down enquiries was temporarily introduced resulting in an increase in the number of orders made (Durham Probation and After-care Service, 1975: p. 34).

The actual involvement of the community service team in the sentencing process varied considerably. In the two pilot areas where schemes were firmly established, their role was far more limited than in the areas with schemes just beginning. Contact was made with the organizer or one of the main-grade probation officers, usually by telephone, and on the basis of the information thus supplied the offender's suitability was determined. In Medway (apart from stand-down enquiries), the availability of a work placement was then confirmed by letter to the probation officer responsible for the preparation of the social enquiry report. In both areas, a member of the community service team would interview the candidate only in borderline cases where very careful assessment was required, as for example where the offender was addicted to drugs or alcohol or thought for other reasons to be highly unstable.

In the areas with schemes just commencing, the procedure was quite different. In Bedford and Ipswich, the probation officer responsible for the preparation of the social enquiry report would contact the community service organizer, who would then arrange to interview the offender. In every case in Bedford and in most cases in Ipswich, if the offender appeared to be a suitable candidate the organizer would also prepare a supplementary report for the court. Furthermore, the organizer or the project officer would usually attend court if the making of an order appeared likely, and was on occasions called to the witness-box to provide further information. In Peterborough and Cambridge, the fact that a member of the community service staff (the project officer) worked from the local probation office facilitated discussion of cases with probation officers, and she herself usually determined suitability after interviewing the candidate. Only difficult decisions, or cases where the project officer did not feel confident enough of her decision, were referred to the community service organizer. The role thus accorded to project officers was in this respect much more extensive than in any other probation area.

It was evident that Nottingham and Medway could not have adopted the procedure of the newer schemes even if they had wanted to, because their current caseloads were far higher. For example, while Nottingham City's current caseload was approaching 300, Ipswich's never rose above twenty in the first year. In any case, the organizers at both Nottingham and Medway believed that the delegation of a large degree of responsibility for assessing community service suitability to area probation officers served a useful educative function. Thus from the beginning of the experimental period they had both encouraged consultation by telephone and, apart from confirming the availability of suitable work, had usually left the final assessment of suitability to field probation officers, although reserving the right to overrule their decisions in exceptional circumstances.

Notwithstanding these variations, in all areas a large part of the responsibility for selecting offenders for community service still rested with the probation officer preparing the social enquiry report. The specialist officer might sometimes point out that the offence was too minor to warrant a custodial sentence, and that community service was therefore not appropriate, or that a probation order might be more suitable, but the field probation officer was not thereby prevented from making a recommendation. He might, for example, simply add in the social enquiry report the ritualized rider commonly found in Nottingham that a community service order would be suitable 'if a custodial sentence is being considered', regardless as to whether or not a custodial sentence appeared likely on the facts of the case. Thus the greater involvement in assessing suitability by the community service team in the areas with newer schemes did not necessarily indicate a more consistent or rational use of the sentence, as the selection of offenders still rested primarily with courts and field probation officers.

Placement in work

The procedure for the placement of offenders in work also varied. The newer schemes generally had placements provisionally arranged for the offender before the order was even made; in Peterborough he had sometimes been introduced already to the voluntary organization for which he later worked. Thus it was not uncommon for an offender to be working during the week-end immediately after the making of the order. In Medway, regular reporting evenings were held at the community service office once a week, and when an offender was made subject to an order, he would be given reporting instructions by the court duty officer. There was thus a minimal delay before the first interview. In Medway also the offender was usually placed with an offender-only work party in the first instance, so that his suitability for more individualized placements with less supervision could be assessed. In Nottingham, the offender was contacted by letter by one of the probation officers in the community service team after the order was made, and instructed to attend the office for an interview. On the basis of that interview, he was then allocated to a particular type of work and, where applicable, introduced to the voluntary organization concerned. There was thus in general a longer delay in Nottingham than in any other area before the first work was performed; at times this could extend to several weeks if the offender was uncooperative.

The selection and organization of work

The diversity and range of tasks and of situations in which offenders are placed make it inaccurate to draw any simplistic distinctions between the nature and organization of work, such as that often made between practical manual tasks and personalized tasks with beneficiaries. In reality, the selection of work involves a choice between several different, though interrelated, alternatives. First, the offender may be placed in a group or he may be given an individual task. Secondly, he may work with other offenders, non-offender voluntary workers, or both; only rarely does a placement involve no contact with other workers. Thirdly, responsibility for supervising offenders may be undertaken directly by the community service team, or it may be delegated to the voluntary or statutory agency concerned, which then files returns with the community service team after each work period and hopefully informs them of any absence by the offender. Supervision by the community service team is often undertaken by supervisors employed on a sessional basis to oversee work parties, especially at week-ends. In Medway, where most offenders were initially placed in a work group, several full-time supervisors were employed. In the areas with schemes just commencing, especially Ipswich, supervision was sometimes undertaken personally by the community service organizer or the project officer. Fourthly, responsibility for determining the precise nature of the task to be performed may be retained by the community service organizer or project officer, or instead be delegated to the voluntary or statutory organization with which the offender is placed. Finally, offenders may be required to do manual tasks or to work personally with individual beneficiaries. However, this is largely an artificial dichotomy, as the two categories sometimes overlap and even merge. Manual work does not preclude close contact with beneficiaries in an informal way, and so-called personalized tasks may include very hard manual labour.

The different combinations of these alternatives make it impossible to represent accurately the full range of tasks performed under the scheme. Work can include, for example: supervising at a youth club; constructional, gardening, or maintenance work at a home for the disabled or elderly; assisting in a hospital, either doing general domestic duties or working personally with patients; nature conservation work; the maintenance of a Scout camp; helping to sort clothes at a second-hand clothing depot; maintenance and repair of a hostel for unmarried mothers; building an adventure playground; and assisting with meals on wheels. Painting, decorating, and gardening for the elderly has been the bread and butter of some community service schemes, which often liaise with Age Concern or Old Age Pensioners' Welfare. In Medway, for example, specialist house painting and decorating groups were kept permanently in being.

There were some differences in principle between the areas

studied here in the approach taken to the selection and organization of work. Nottingham allowed the offender, as far as possible, to choose the type of work he would perform and although he might sometimes be persuaded to change his mind, the community service team accepted his final choice unless risk factors precluded it. Although in other areas, too, the offender was permitted to state his preference, these were not always followed. Ipswich gave the offender little choice; and Bedford, Peterborough, and Cambridge were prepared to override the offender's choice if their assessment of his treatment needs pointed to the desirability of a different type of placement. Medway gave the offender more choice as his order progressed. Apart from Nottingham, therefore, there were many cases in which no real effort was made to ensure that the offender would value his contribution to the community through community service, or that the needs of the beneficiary were those with which he could readily identify.

All areas placed emphasis upon the fostering of social responsibility, particularly by the enhancement of self-respect. In some schemes, this has created a preference for individual rather than group placements. In Essex no groups were reportedly used for the first six months of the scheme, and subsequently they were used only when the supply of individual placements dried up. However, the areas studied here were not so rigid; group and individual placements both played a part. Nor were practical manual tasks given less weight than personalized ones; indeed, there was a healthy questioning of a value system which automatically assumes that manual work and the skills associated with it are less rewarding and less beneficial than working person to person. Probation officers in the Nottingham community service team observed:

> Practical work placements, if carefully selected, can provide the offender with a very direct way of carrying out a helping role in the community, together with the opportunity to see and feel whatever gratitude is felt by the person or people he has been working for. If well set up, the practical placement can encompass considerable flexibility, which allows the offender, not only the chance to use his practical skill, but at the same time to relate to people on a personal level in all kinds of ways. (Ringrose *et al.*, 1975)

There were, however, clear differences in the value attached to other aspects of the rehabilitative philosophy of the community service order. In Ipswich, a continuing relationship with the community service team rather than a beneficiary or voluntary organization was believed to be essential; thus offenders were often shifted from task to task as a matter of policy, so that they could experience and learn to adjust to more than one type of community service work. This was facilitated in Ipswich by the fact that the community service team supervised the offenders more closely than in any other area. On the other hand, the wish to encourage the development of new talents and interests, and to utilize the potential value of 'New Careers', meant that (in Nottingham in particular) offenders placed with voluntary or statutory organizations were left as far as possible with the same organization throughout the order, so that a sense of involvement and commitment might be created.

There were also significant differences between areas which were not attributable to variations in policy, but to practical constraints which dictated what type of work was performed. This meant that the nature of the work was sometimes related only tenuously to the organizer's view of what was theoretically desirable. For example, even if the offender was in principle permitted to choose his task—as in Nottingham—practical exigencies might prevent this choice from being accepted.

The first of these practical constraints was the risk that the offender appeared to present. This was partly determined by the nature of his offending; the range of placements available for certain violent and sexual offenders, for example, was inevitably limited. However, it was also related to his response to the order in terms of co-operation, punctuality, and standard of work. Strict supervision, usually in groups, was necessary in all areas to cater for the hard core of difficult offenders who inevitably presented themselves. Nottingham, Medway, and Peterborough each had an added facility in the form of a community service workshop, developed for the nucleus of high-risk, disruptive, or uncooperative workers who could not be trusted to complete their orders satisfactorily in an outside placement. In these workshops, offenders worked under a sessional supervisor on carpentry projects, sometimes making wooden toys for handicapped children, or building playground equipment. In Nottingham it operated for five days a week; in Peterborough for only two evenings a week. Sometimes, too, a workshop was the only appropriate placement for an unreliable and virtually unemployable offender for whom community service was being used as a means of developing a work habit. The areas without such workshops were usually unable to find any suitable work at all for these offenders.

Secondly, difficulties of travel often arose, especially with offenders living in rural communities. A lack of regular public transport might at worst preclude the making of an order altogether; at best it could severely limit the choice of the time and place of work.

Thirdly, areas with smaller caseloads paradoxically confronted difficulties not experienced by those with larger caseloads. Particularly in areas with schemes just commencing, commitments were made to organizations that proved difficult to meet without a regular flow of orders. Placements were sometimes determined largely or completely by the need to maintain the goodwill of organizations by keeping promises that work would be done. The larger caseloads of Nottingham and Medway therefore permitted far more flexibility in placing an individual offender.

Fourthly, the structure and organization of voluntary agencies played a vital part in the development of the scheme in all areas. Nottingham had a strong tradition of voluntary service—one of the reasons for its choice as an experimental area. Other areas had less developed voluntary organizations that were often hollow in the middle, in the sense that they were aware of needs but did not have the resources to cope with them. Community service by offenders was a means of filling the gap, so that, as in Medway, voluntary organizations were stronger and better structured as a result. However, co-operation with the scheme was far from universal. Certain established middle-class organizations, like the Red Cross and the W.R.V.S., were reluctant to participate and only cautiously accepted that offenders might have a contribution to make. There was also opposition from some statutory service organizations. Even when there was no real objection, it often took some time for official approval to be given. Thus, for example, of twenty-eight agencies used in Peterborough during the first six months of the scheme, only two were statutory organizations. There was particular hostility in all areas from hospitals, partly because in a large bureaucracy a certain person or group at some level was always likely to object. Unions, for example, were sometimes afraid that voluntary labour would be used as a form of economy and thus heighten the chances of redundancy. The time taken to break down such oppositions was a major factor in determining what placements were available.

The co-operation and organization of voluntary and statutory agencies also partly determined the extent to which responsibility for supervision of an individual placement was delegated to them. In Nottingham and Medway, it was quite common for a trusted voluntary organization to determine the work the offender should do, to negotiate with him when the work should be done, and to refer the case to the community service team only to file work returns or report some problem. In Medway spot checks were carried out to ensure that no collusion between the offender and the voluntary organization was occurring. This degree of delegation was rare in the areas with newer schemes. In Cambridge, the organizer felt that he had to specify the type and time of work in order to prevent manipulation of the organization by the worker.

The fifth practical consideration was the staffing of the community service team and the resources available to it. In Bedford, at a time when less than fifteen offenders were engaged in community service work, a sessional supervisor was employed to organize the building of a fishing platform on a lakeside at a home for seriously disabled youngsters. From then on, his employment was continued and offenders were allocated to group tasks, including the clearance of a churchyard, when they might otherwise have been placed individually. (It is, of course, possible to employ sessional supervisors only for such time as they are strictly needed but this was not done.) In the same way, a workshop, once created, had to be used; in Peterborough it was felt that four or five offenders in a workshop were needed to make the employment of its supervisor economical.

Finally, the level of unemployment was a minor influence upon the work which was generally available. It was accepted from the outset that the work performed under a community service order should be work which would not otherwise have been done, so that it did not interfere with opportunities for paid employment. The Home Office Working Group recognized that the co-operation of the trade union movement would be essential to the success of the scheme. While the Trades Union Congress gave its official blessing, there were nevertheless problems, for example with hospitals. It is, of course, almost impossible at times to distinguish between the work of paid staff and the work done by volunteers. As it seems likely that at least 20,000 orders a year will be made when the scheme is extended to all areas, its effect on the staffing levels of statutory agencies in particular cannot be ignored. At a time of high national unemployment, therefore, this was clearly a factor, albeit a minor one, in determining what work an offender, or indeed any volunteer, was permitted to perform.

These practical constraints not only modify policy but also bear upon the type of offender on whom the community service order is imposed. The existence of workshops, or of many practical work groups under strict supervision, may enable the acceptance of a greater number of serious or high-risk offenders for whom suitable individual placements would not be available. Conversely, the need to show caution so that public confidence in the scheme is not jeopardized may result in the rejection of offenders who might otherwise have been suitable.

The administration of the scheme by the probation service

The Wootton Committee did not automatically assume that the probation service was the most suitable agency to undertake the administration of community service. It considered several alternatives—local authorities, voluntary organizations, the prison service, and the police. It was thought, however, that local authorities might have difficulty in handling the inevitable fluctuation in the number of offenders available for community service work, and the Committee did not have reliable evidence of the character and efficiency of voluntary agencies. Likewise, it was believed that neither the police nor the prison service had the organization, resources, or knowledge of local conditions needed to administer such a scheme. Thus the Committee concluded that the task had to be delegated to the probation service. This would give the service a novel function: indeed, the Committee was initially sceptical of its willingness to undertake the discipline and control which responsibility for the scheme would entail. The Home Office Working Group also wondered whether a scheme of a punitive nature might compromise the traditional image of the probation and after-care service as a helping and treating agency, and for that reason advocated a wide variety of tasks without an overtly penal element.

However, despite some misgivings by individual probation officers, the service as a whole did not object to this extension of their existing functions. There was, for example, no concerted opposition of the type which greeted the publication of the Younger Report (Home Office, 1974), which advocated stricter requirements and sanctions for the supervision of young adult offenders.[2] Most officers were content to wait and observe how the sentence developed. The reason was clear: the community service order was welcomed because it was perceived primarily as a rehabilitative measure. Thus the general orientation of the probation service in favour of a predominantly treatment approach emerged at the outset. The diverse philosophies to which the sentence appealed enabled the service to undertake its new role without compromising its image as a treatment agency. It was not so much that community service was recognized as a less onerous penalty than imprisonment and therefore an acceptable sphere for involvement on that basis; it was rather that its penal content was conveniently relegated to the background.

But this was not the whole story. Other pressures were also operating to ensure that the punitive aspect of the sentence was not entirely forgotten. First, some probation officers, particularly those responsible for organizing the schemes, were concerned to utilize community service as a means of reducing the prison population. Thus they accepted its punitive aim because it was less potentially destructive than imprisonment. In the social enquiry reports studied here, the term 'constructive penalty' recurred time and again. Secondly, the fact that the sentence achieved some tangible result in the form of work which was supposed to benefit society, gave it an appeal independent of rehabilitative objectives. It has been argued, for example, that the community service order is appropriate as a punishment for some offenders who continue to reoffend, whatever its effect as a treatment might be (West, 1976: p. 73).

These pressures found expression in the belief of some areas, including Nottingham, that its value as an alternative to imprisonment could be exploited to the full only if the coercive and punitive elements embodied in it were given expression. The six pilot areas were evenly divided on this issue. Three, including Kent, felt that it should have a wider use and be available in cases where it appeared appropriate to the needs of the offender, notwithstanding that a custodial sentence might not otherwise have been imposed.

Thus ambivalence and ambiguity have been engendered. This is not only reflected in a division between the use of the sentence by the courts as a tariff measure[3] and its use as an individualized measure (which will be described in detail later) but also in the resolution of several issues arising in the practical administration of the scheme.

First, the widespread incidence of unemployment among those sentenced to a community service order raises the question: when should work under such an order be performed? Unless it is undertaken only during normal leisure time, it may lose much of its penal element. On the other hand, as a means of developing a work habit, it needs to be undertaken regularly during normal employment hours. Should an unemployed offender, therefore, be allowed to perform the requisite number of hours quickly by working on weekdays, or should his work be restricted to evenings and weekends so that he does not have an unfair advantage over employed offenders?

This issue was never fully resolved by the areas studied here. The only restriction upon the number of hours which could be worked during any one week was an informal national agreement with the Department of Employment that unemployed offenders be left with two clear weekdays in which to sign on at the local employment offices and look for work. Apart from this, Nottingham and Bedford made little attempt to restrict the number of hours worked per week. In Bedford one order of 120 hours was completed in five weeks. Another unemployed offender stated in interview that he had no intention of doing community service work at week-ends after a week's employment; thus he ceased to look seriously for a job until he had completed the order. He performed 120 hours' work in under three months, working for three weekdays per week. In Nottingham one offender did 140 hours of a 240-hour order in three weeks, and another did 42 hours of a 100-hour order in one week. Other areas attempted some restriction, but were nevertheless prepared to make exceptions on rehabilitative grounds. In Peterborough, for example, a 200-hour order was recommended with the specific intention that the offender should work during the week to establish a work pattern; she completed the order in two months as a domestic help at an old people's home.

Some variation and flexibility in work instructions is, of course, inevitable. On the one hand, this is due to the need to cater for offenders on shift work. On the other, it stems from the fact that some work provided by outside organizations requires regular workers—perhaps for several days a week. But the ambiguity in objectives magnifies the variation, illustrating that the pursuit of rehabilitation can seriously dilute the penal character of the sentence.

Secondly, the clash between penal requirements and the offender's needs is reflected in the issue of control. Individualized considerations can lead to lenient treatment which militates against the exaction of a proper penalty. In the areas studied here, this often resulted from a recognition by the community service organizer of an offender's problems, e.g. domestic conflict, irregular work habits, depression:

> In Ipswich, a young adult offender completed a community service order after eighteen unacceptable absences. He was breached once after twelve absences, resulting in a fine of £25 and continuance of the order. The organizer's final summary stated, 'His response continued to be unsatisfactory, but because we knew of his many personal problems he was persevered with in spite of repeated absences.'

On other occasions, failure to initiate breach proceedings appeared to be the consequence of an extreme reluctance on the part of the organizer and also the court to take punitive action while there was still some vestige of hope that the order might be completed:

> In Peterborough, one order of 240 hours took one month short of two years to complete. During that time the offender, a male aged between 17 and 20, failed to comply with work instructions at least thirty times. In two separate proceedings for breach he was fined and the order was

continued. In addition, the order was twice extended upon application
by the community service organizer.

It was evident that there were no consistent principles, either within
or between areas, for determining the appropriate point for initia-
tion of breach proceedings. The perceived need to pay due regard
to individualized factors, and to give the offender as much opportunity as possible to respond to the order by becoming involved in
voluntary work, militated against the formulation of such principles. Thus organizers could to some extent manipulate their
'success' rate, in the eyes of the court, by tolerating more unacceptable absenteeism and avoiding the need for breach proceedings in
some cases. Moreover, some courts themselves were prepared to be
excessively lenient in particular cases, as the above example in
Peterborough indicates.

Thirdly, the ambiguity in objectives is of course of direct relevance to the type of action taken by courts when breach of an order
is proved. The diverse approach to the sentence means that this
action may be far from predictable. It is possible, for example, that
a community service order may be imposed for rehabilitative rather
than penal or tariff reasons, but that a later court may impose a
custodial sentence for breach in the belief that the original sentence
had been imposed as an alternative to custody. The reverse may
also be true. In either case, the basis for the court decision may
have little to do with the reasons why breach action is initiated by
the community service organizer. The scope for inconsistency both
within and between areas and courts is enormous.

Of course, not all such inconsistencies can be explained solely in
terms of differences in objectives. For example, inadequate staffing
resources can severely limit the feasibility of control. In Nottingham, a low staff–client ratio for a prolonged period, which gave
the probation officers in the community service team a current
caseload of about eighty, meant that offenders were allowed considerable latitude. Probation officers tended to turn their attention
first towards the need to arrange placements for co-operative
offenders; only when time allowed did they turn their attention to
the absentees.[4] This was hardly surprising, since a community
service caseload, unlike a probation caseload, carries with it
constant pressure to place new offenders in work, to shift existing
offenders to a different work placement where necessary, and to
ensure that promises of work to the statutory and voluntary organizations participating in the scheme are being met.

Moreover the nature of the work placement also affects the
control which can be applied to an offender. A breach of a

community service order, especially if contested, is both more difficult to prove and requires a greater investment of time than a breach of a probation order. Particular problems arise when an offender is supervised by the agency with which he is placed:

> If the probation service administering community service is reluctant to involve the agencies in acting as witnesses in revocation [i.e. breach] proceedings (and most are, as are most work-providing agencies to act in this capacity), it is likely to be the case that offenders working for voluntary agencies will have more unsatisfactory failures to attend before revocation proceedings occur, because they will have to absent themselves sufficiently frequently from the work site to draw the attention of the community service organizer, and to provide enough testable events for revocation proceedings in court. (Pease and West, 1977: p. 19)

It is thus often necessary to transfer an offender who has repeatedly failed to comply with work instructions to a group placement under the supervision of a sessional supervisor before breach proceedings can be initiated. In any case, it was standard practice in all areas studied here to instruct the offender to attend at least one different placement before taking out a summons for breach. For this reason, some offenders with up to twelve unacceptable (although not necessarily consecutive) absences had been no more than threatened with breach proceedings.

Despite such practical constraints, it is clear that variations are usually attributable, at least in part, to the ambivalence in the objectives of the community service order, and that clearer agreement on the purposes for which it is being imposed would obviate many of the difficulties.

Not all of the blame for the continuance of this ambivalence, however, rests with the probation service. The community service organizer is dependent in his job upon the support and co-operation of other agencies apart from his colleagues in the service. Thus his objectives in administering the scheme are to some extent tempered by the demands of others outside the service. The largely insular and protected interaction between probation officer and offender characteristic of the probation order cannot be sustained, because the offender is carrying out his prescribed tasks in the community, often with other non-offender voluntary workers who may or may not know that he is an offender. Thus community attitudes, and the need for the scheme to maintain a good public image, dictate to a much greater degree than in a probation order the manner in which the sentence is implemented. In other words, community service schemes entail a complex interaction between organizers and others both within and outside the probation service, and this sometimes leads to strain and conflict. However the organizer wishes the sentence to be used and administered, his own personal philosophy will be modified by the need to take account of the views of others; hence he 'must have the capacity to sit on a number of diverging fences' (West, 1976: p. 69), to attempt the impossible task of reconciling irreconcilable objectives and views.

The absence of practical guidelines

The absence of national practical guidelines has encouraged the lack of uniformity between areas. Few directives have been issued by the Home Office on the administration of community service schemes. Such circulars as have been issued have concentrated on legal provisions, and the criteria and procedure for selection of offenders. Thus local probation areas have been largely free to develop their own policies on issues of practical administration without the need to achieve uniformity or consistency of approach on a national level. The Powers of Criminal Courts Act 1973 (s. 48) empowers the Secretary of State to make rules about arrangements for work and its performance. The Under-Secretary of State, in debating the original legislation, stated:

> There are four aspects about which the Secretary of State will have to lay down general rules to cover work with community service. It is obviously necessary that there should be similar arrangements throughout the country with regard to the keeping of records, the reckoning of time actually worked, and ensuring that it is actually done. (H.C. Debates, Standing Committee G, 10/2/72)

Despite this 'obvious necessity', no such rules have yet been made.

There has been some degree of liaison and exchange of ideas on an informal basis between community service organizers of different areas, and some new schemes have attempted to model themselves on one or other of the pilot schemes. This reciprocal dissemination of approaches and ideas, however, has been haphazard, and wide variations exist on many practical issues. Differences occur, for example, in the procedure for the assessment and selection of offenders for a community service order, the allowance of travelling time and lunch-breaks as hours worked, and the payment of travelling and other expenses. Some discrepancies are glaring. For example, Middlesex operated a practical assessment programme involving the community service candidate in a community project during the remand period, and then made an assessment of his suitability on the basis of his response. This created difficulties for those outside courts unfamiliar with the practice if they wanted to impose an order on an offender residing in that area. It also resulted in injustice on occasions. An offender, for example, might work voluntarily on two occasions, be declared suitable, and then be sent to prison by a later bench who thought a community service order too lenient. Kent, too, operated its own policy of awarding bonus incentive hours for good conduct to an offender subject to an order, by deducting perhaps eight hours from the total hours outstanding. This was usually done about half-way through a medium or long order with an offender who had had no more than one or two unacceptable absences, and whose work performance had been good. It was a policy without parallel in any other area studied here.

There are four reasons for this apparent lack of any attempt to achieve over-all uniformity. The first and most obvious reason is the deliberate ambivalence on the purposes of the sentence already discussed. The second reason is inherent in the nature of the probation service. Probation officers have traditionally retained considerable discretion to utilize their 'professional' skills in the best way they think fit. They might therefore have resisted attempts to have uniformity imposed from above. Thirdly, the deliberate policy in the experimental period had been to allow the pilot areas as much elasticity as possible, so that the utility of different approaches could be observed. With the extension of the scheme to all areas, this approach has continued. Some of the experience of the pilot areas has been communicated to new schemes by way of advice, but this has been on specific issues. No over-all strategy has been apparent. The final reason for this failure to implement a rational and consistent policy is the perceived need for flexibility to cater for local conditions. The community service order, more than any other sentence of the court, is dependent for its success on community involvement, co-operation, and on particular local characteristics such as transport facilities; the nature of the scheme which evolves is therefore bound to vary from area to area. Griffiths observes that 'the consequent flexibility of the scheme is one of its strongest points, permitting as it does the exploitation of local opportunities and encouraging an attempt to contribute towards the satisfaction of local needs' (Griffiths, 1977: p. 269). To some extent this is true, but the resulting local autonomy has created discrepancies which clearly extend far beyond the need to take account of local conditions. Flexibility is obviously needed in the choice of tasks and the way in which they are performed. Variations more open to criticism are decisions about breach actions; practices relating to the assessment and selection

of offenders for community service; and the payment of travelling expenses and awarding of travelling time, to take but a few
examples.

Part Two

THE USE OF THE COMMUNITY SERVICE
ORDER BY THE COURTS

5

The method of research

The initial expectation that the community service order would serve a valuable function in diverting offenders from custodial sentences is, of course, wholly dependent upon the way in which the courts use the sentence. In this study[1] the sentencing practice of six magistrates' courts was closely examined, both to determine the over-all extent to which the sentence was being used and the types of offenders upon which it was being imposed, and also to highlight variations in sentencing practice between courts.

Magistrates' courts were selected in preference to Crown Courts for three main reasons. First, it was unlikely that the community service order would frequently be used as a substitute for medium or long terms of imprisonment; it was therefore anticipated that its use would be concentrated mainly within magistrates' courts. The experience of the pilot areas had been entirely consistent with this expectation. For example, the Home Office Research Unit reported that during the first eighteen months of the scheme, up until the end of June 1974, almost 74 per cent of orders had been imposed by magistrates' courts (Pease et al., 1975: p. 28). In any case, the bulk of indictable offences are dealt with by magistrates' courts, and thus it was expected that a greater number of community service orders would be imposed by them than by Crown Courts. Secondly, there was less difficulty in gaining access to records in magistrates' courts. Thirdly, and perhaps most important, it would have been difficult, if not impossible, to find six Crown Courts, geographically convenient and all of the same tier, which had community service schemes available in their areas. Crown Courts of different tiers could obviously not be compared because, by definition, they deal with offences of different degrees of seriousness.

The study was undertaken during 1976 and 1977. The limited number of courts with community service orders available to them at this time severely restricted the choice of courts. Two courts—Nottingham and Medway—were selected from the pilot areas. The other four—Ipswich, Peterborough, Cambridge, and Bedford—

were selected from areas with schemes just commencing. This provided some basis for comparison between courts in areas with established schemes and those in areas with new schemes. Peterborough and Cambridge were deliberately selected from the same probation area in the hope that, in comparing their sentencing practice, the influence of the community service organizer and the nature of the scheme being administered could be eliminated. Unfortunately this hope was disappointed, since a new organizer took over in Cambridge at a point when the data collection in Peterborough was nearing completion and that in Cambridge, whose scheme was launched nine months later, was just beginning.

The investigation of sentencing practice took the form of a comparison of the characteristics of a sample of offenders given a community service order, imprisonment, a suspended sentence, a probation order, or a detention centre order.[2] In this way a picture was built up of the relationship between the application of the community service order and that of four other sentences which might be regarded as somewhere near it in the penal scale. The sample was obtained by taking from the court register all offenders given any of these sentences during a period of twelve months in each court. The total number of offenders included in this sample amounted to 2,021, of whom 308 received a community service order.

Since it was important to study the use of the community service order when the scheme was at the same stage of development in each of the four courts where it was first being utilized, the periods did not coincide chronologically. The cases in Nottingham and Medway were taken for the period of twelve months beginning 1 June 1975. Those from the other courts were collected for twelve months from the first date of the availability of the community service order in those courts, which ranged from 1 April 1975 to 1 April 1976.

Disparity in sentencing

The description of the use of a particular sentence immediately raises the fundamental question of sentencing disparity: to what extent did the sentencing practices of different courts appear to be inconsistent with each other; and in particular, what variations occurred in the use of the community service order.

Sentencing disparity, which refers to the existence of an unjustifiable inconsistency between courts in their use of different sentences, has been the main focus of past research into sentencing practice.[3] The principal concern has been to discover how far variations between courts can be attributed to the attitudes of the particular sentencer and his individual sentencing habits. However, these studies have usually done little to clarify what consistency actually means, or in what circumstances inconsistency becomes unjustifiable.

It is easier to state what consistency does not mean, than to provide a single definition of what it does mean. First, it does not merely mean equality of consideration; it requires not only that similar general considerations be taken into account, but that relevant factors be given equal weight in the determination of the correct sentence in different cases. Secondly, consistency is not synonymous with justice, in other than a formal sense. Equality of treatment has played a greater part in some definitions of justice than others. Those in the Aristotelian tradition, for example, have seen it as the most basic principle of justice. However, as Ginsberg has pointed out, a distinction must be drawn between formal or procedural justice and substantive justice (Ginsberg, 1965: p. 7). The formal character of justice requires that it be impartially applied according to the same general principles (a concept closely akin to equality and consistency), while the substance of justice governs what should be done by, for, or to equals or unequals. Thus consistency does not necessarily produce substantive justice, and it could be argued that one just sentence and one unjust one are better than two sentences which are both unjust but consistent. But the fact is that there is notoriously little agreement on what constitutes substantive justice. Moreover, justice is a concept which is, at least to some degree, relative to time and place; even when it is defined according to natural right, it is not absolute or immutable. Consistency therefore provides a convenient alternative criterion by which the sentencing practice of different courts can be assessed and compared.

However, the definition of consistency depends upon the perspective from which sentences are being adjudged. Since no two cases are exactly alike in all respects, it is essential to specify the elements in respect of which consistency should be observed. Under a sentencing structure embodying elements of retributive punishment, consistency would require that individuals convicted of similar offences in similar circumstances should attract similar dispositions, subject to some allowance for mitigating factors. Under an individualized sentencing structure, on the other hand, the measure of consistency would be quite different: it might take elements related to the offender's needs, or to the risk that he would reoffend.

The presumption of a tariff

The major theoretical perspective from which the five selected sentences were compared here was that of a sentencing tariff. A 'tariff' sentence is a sentence chosen in the light of the gravity of the offence in relation to other offences in the criminal calendar and in relation to other examples of the same type of offence. It is thus a set of conventions used by courts as a method of achieving some consistency and rationality in the sentencing of different cases.

The tariff cannot be equated with any particular sentencing objective. It embodies a whole range of penal theories: retribution, general and individual deterrence, denunciation, protection of the public, and even expiation. The choice of a sentence on a tariff basis also does not necessarily conflict with the belief or hope that that sentence can serve a rehabilitative purpose. However, the essence of the tariff is the principle of proportionality. In so far, therefore, as any of these objectives override that principle by requiring a more severe or less severe sentence than is demanded by it, to that extent they are inconsistent with the tariff.

A sentencing tariff has at least two distinct but clearly related elements. One refers to a *scale* of penalties, over all offence categories, ranked according to their inherent severity. This scale may be either reflected in a choice between different sentences—for example, between a conditional discharge, a fine, or a sentence of imprisonment—or it may be expressed in the application of different degrees of a particular penalty—for example the amount of a fine or the length of a prison sentence.

Once this scale of penalties is established, a second element requires the fixing of a normal *range* of penalties for a certain category of offence which operates as a guide to courts in deciding what the appropriate sentence for a particular instance of that offence should be. For example, in determining the proper length of a prison sentence for an offence of rape, the application of tariff principles would require the court to examine the appropriate distribution of all sentences of imprisonment for rape, and then to fix the length of the sentence so as to reflect the seriousness of the instant offence in relation to the whole spectrum of offences of rape.

Since the concern here is to locate the community service order in the sentencing structure according to its relationship to other sentences over the whole range of offences dealt with by magistrates' courts, the tariff perspective refers to the scale of penalties operating in magistrates' courts, as reflected in a choice between different sentences, rather than the range of penalties applicable to any particular type of offence.

The applicability of tariff principles to the sentencing practice of higher courts has been thoroughly demonstrated by Thomas (1978) in his analysis of the sentencing policy of the Court of Appeal (Criminal Division). For example, wide disparity between sentences imposed on co-defendants or on offenders convicted of essentially similar crimes may be grounds for an appeal against sentence by the offender on whom the more severe sentence is imposed (*R.* v. *Heyes*, [1974] Crim. L.R. 57, *R.* v. *Street*, [1974] Crim. L.R. 264.) In *R.* v. *Ford*, [1969] 1 W.L.R. 1703 it was held that:

> In relation to offences of dishonesty, sentences of imprisonment— except where there is an element of protection of the public involved— are normally intended to be *the correct sentence for the particular crime*, and not to include a curative element [my emphasis].

Similar statements have been made in *R.* v. *Coombs*, [1973] Crim. L.R. 65 and *R.* v. *Jenkins*, [1977] Crim. L.R. 49 in relation to the use of imprisonment as a protective measure. Many other examples can be cited to support the proposition that as a general rule the Court of Appeal (Criminal Division) operates on the basis that the sentence should be proportionate to the seriousness of the offence.

The presumption of a set of similar principles in magistrates' courts cannot be validated by reference to empirical research. However, observation suggests that a tariff approach is also firmly entrenched in the sentencing policy of magistrates' courts; any attempt to describe the use of a sentence, therefore, is best undertaken from a tariff perspective. The presumption of such a tariff, however, does not imply that the principles are uniform throughout all magistrates' courts. The Court of Appeal (Criminal Division) is the guardian of consistency in higher courts, but the principles it enunciates are unlikely to have much influence on magisterial sentencing policy. In any case, as Thomas has pointed out, since only the offender is able to initiate an appeal against sentence, the Court of Appeal's 'opportunities for refining the principles governing sentences for minor offences are limited, and it has less chance to deal with distinctions between non-custodial measures such as probation and discharge than with the principles affecting the length of sentences of imprisonment' (Thomas, 1978: ch. 1). Moreover, there is no regular procedure by which the results of appeals to Crown Courts against sentence are relayed back to the sentencing magistrates. It is thus possible that each magistrates' court operates according to a tariff scale peculiar to itself, a scale which might have little or no regard to what is done in neighbouring courts of the same kind. In other words, a tariff scale might achieve some consistency within a court, while leaving wide discrepancies between different courts.

The idea of a tariff has sometimes been rejected because it suggests a spurious precision of calculation which is misleading. For example, the term has occasionally been used to imply a ready reckoner such as the structure of basic road traffic penalties for minor motoring offences suggested to magistrates by the Magistrates' Association in 1965 (which, subject to later revision, is still in use in many magistrates' courts). These standard penalties were intended to be regarded as the appropriate norm for an ordinary or average offender which should be increased or reduced only in the light of unusual aggravating or mitigating factors. It is this idea of an exact penalty which can be determined more or less mechanically, once all the basic facts about the offence and the offender are known, which Blom-Cooper presumably had in mind when he referred to 'the notional tariff' (Blom-Cooper, 1976: p. 6). Any idea of a tariff applicable in this sense to general sentencing policy has been firmly resisted by the judiciary, which has often been at pains to stress that there is 'no scientific precision involved in deciding on the correct sentence' (Walker and Giller, 1977: p. 112).

In this study, the description of sentencing practice from a tariff perspective does not imply the existence of such a mechanical scale or rigid set of rules. Instead, it should be taken to presume the existence of a flexible and somewhat imprecise framework which courts use as a general guide. This does not mean that there is only one correct penalty in any given situation and that any other penalty would be wrong, nor does it exclude consideration of a host of personal and situational factors which can assist in selecting an appropriate sentence. As Thomas has put it:

> The principles of the tariff constitute a framework by reference to which the sentencer can determine what factors in a particular case are relevant to his decision and what weight should be attached to each of them. Properly used, they offer a basis for maintaining consistency in the sentencing of different offenders, while observing relevant distinctions, making appropriate allowances for individual factors and preserving adequate scope for the exercise of judicial discretion. (Thomas, 1978: ch. 2)

Of course, tariff principles are not the only considerations taken into account by courts in imposing sentences. Since the end of the nineteenth century, penal measures, both custodial and non-custodial, have evolved and been administered, in theory, with the specific aim of changing the offender's attitudes and way of life by rehabilitating rather than simply punishing him. Initially this was not reflected to any large extent in sentencing practice. Individualized treatment was simply regarded as complementary to a system of penalties fixed according to the seriousness of the offence. Thus the Gladstone Committee (Departmental Committee on Prisons 1895) stressed the reformative purposes of sentencing, but implied that if the system was properly regulated there was no contradiction between these and other considerations; and in 1932, despite the fact that the probation order had been in existence for a quarter of a century, the Departmental Committee on Persistent Offenders felt able to describe the general principles of sentencing almost exclusively in terms of a tariff.

It appears that the characteristics of offenders were to be taken into account, not for the purpose of assessing the needs of the offender, but rather as mitigating factors which might depreciate the seriousness of the particular offence. The needs of the offender would be taken care of during the implementation of the sentence chosen; the actual choice had to be governed by other factors. Thus little attempt was made to synthesize individualized and tariff considerations into a coherent whole; a synthesis was thought to have been achieved already. The introduction of individualized measures such as the probation order, which were designed to cater for the needs of the offender and solely directed towards his rehabilitation, were initially reserved for relatively minor and first offenders and thus interfered little with the over-all tariff structure.

Increasingly, however, the picture has been blurred during the course of this century by the growing influence of individualized considerations, the development of more non-custodial measures, and their extension to more serious offenders. This has been accompanied by some recognition of the tension that may arise from an attempt to reconcile different and sometimes competing sentencing objectives. The Streatfeild Committee, for example, thought that the tariff system was not always congruous with rehabilitative considerations:

As [the rehabilitative] side of sentencing has developed, it has been found that in individual cases these other considerations sometimes suggest a different sentence from the one which would have been imposed under the 'tariff system' and also that one objective may suggest a different sentence from another. Sentencers have to resolve these competing claims and decide which consideration should be dominant in a particular case. . . . In short, sentencing is becoming a more complex task. . . . In a considerable, and growing, number of cases the 'tariff system' can no longer be relied upon to fit all the considerations in the court's mind. (Interdepartmental Committee on the Business of the Criminal Courts, 1961: para. 260)

Thomas, too, found a conflict between different sentencing objectives. He postulated a dual system of sentencing in the Court of Appeal (Criminal Division), whereby a policy decision is made in each individual case between a tariff measure fixed by reference to the gravity of the offence and an individualized measure determined exclusively by reference to the characteristics and needs of the offender.

An individualized sentencing model has therefore been grafted on to the traditional tariff model, and the two exist in an uneasy alliance. Although the tariff has retained its significance, it is now sometimes subordinated to the requirements of rehabilitation, usually in the direction of a less severe sentence. For instance, in a magistrates' court an alcoholic, whose avowed intention of overcoming his drinking problem is believed or who is thought likely to respond to treatment despite a lack of strong motivation, may be given a probation order with a condition of residence or psychiatric treatment, instead of the prison sentence which otherwise might have been expected on tariff principles. Sexual offences with a strong compulsive element also frequently attract a probation order, despite the existence of a lengthy previous record or the failure of earlier attempts at treatment. Thomas also cites the example of the 'intermediate recidivist', typically a male between the ages of 20 and 40 with a long history of crime and institutional experience, who is not yet totally institutionalized and whose situation suggests that he might respond to an individualized measure. In such cases the courts have sometimes been willing to overlook the demands of the tariff.[4]

Nevertheless, although analytically one can perceive such a dual system of sentencing in operation, there is a closer relationship between individualized and tariff measures than is sometimes realized. First, some sentences are used as both, notably Borstal training and the detention centre order. The tariff location of these sentences according to their perceived severity inevitably reflects the fact that they are sometimes used as an individualized measure; in such cases no clear-cut dividing line can always be discerned between what is tariff and what is individualized. This is particularly so in the use of the detention centre order by magistrates' courts.

Secondly, it appears that some sentences, although clearly individualized, are occasionally used as a tariff measure because there is no appropriate alternative which can properly reflect the serious (or minor) nature of the offence. Thus, for example, a probation order may be imposed because the financial situation of the offender rules out a fine as a feasible alternative, a conditional discharge is perceived to be too lenient, and a suspended sentence is perceived to be too severe. Consistent with this hypothesis is the finding in this study that in twenty-one cases which attracted a probation order the social enquiry report categorically stated that such a measure would be entirely inappropriate. For example, in Nottingham, the social enquiry report on an offender who received a two-year probation order stated:

> The officer who supervised Mr X previously experienced a complete lack of response on his part with frequent missed appointments. . . . It is difficult to make any constructive recommendation in view of Mr X's failure to report but it seems that he is not prepared to co-operate with the Department and a probation order does not seem appropriate.

This may sometimes have been due to a belief by the magistrates that they were better judges of treatment potential than the probation officer, but their adherence to tariff principles in imposing some of these orders was strongly indicated. Thus, for example, in Bedford three co-defendants received two-year probation orders, although in two of the cases the probation officer felt this to be inappropriate because the offenders were lacking in motivation. Since a probation order was recommended for the third defendant, there was a clear implication that the court felt it could not impose different sentences on defendants with similar backgrounds and previous records who were convicted of the same offences.

Thirdly, the primary policy decision between a tariff and an individualized rehabilitative measure is itself partly determined by the gravity of the offence. The more serious an offence is perceived to be, the more reluctant the court will be to impose a more lenient rehabilitative measure than that indicated by the tariff. West (1976) has suggested that whether this reluctance can be overcome depends upon two factors, 'effectiveness' and 'fault'. The less the perceived degree of culpability by the offender, the more permissible a treatment option becomes. But the treatment measure must also hold out some hope of effectiveness. Thus the more serious the offence or the more culpable the offender, the greater must be the likelihood of effectiveness.

Despite the fact, therefore, that the tariff has been modified to some extent by individualized considerations, a description of the use of a sentence from a tariff perspective is a valuable exercise in reflecting its position in the scale of penalties, since it is this position which will determine its viability as a sentence for the more serious offender.

The choice of characteristics for comparison

The offence and offender characteristics selected for comparison
were therefore those which were thought appropriate to indicate
the use of each sentence from a tariff perspective and to link it to a
scale of penalties. These factors reflected three dimensions.

First, information was collected on the nature and number of
offences leading to conviction, and the number of offences taken
into consideration, at the current court appearance, thus allowing
some estimation of the gravity of the offence. However, an
accurate evaluation of this was difficult. Apart from noting the
value of property involved in the commission of property crimes,
the nature of the offences leading to conviction was defined in the
records solely in terms of their legal categories. Furthermore, for
the sake of simplicity of analysis it was possible to note the nature
of only the most serious offence. However, these limitations may
not be a serious handicap. As magistrates' courts deal with the
more minor indictable offences and all non-indictable offences,
variations in the nature of offences are unlikely to be as great as
those encountered at Crown Court level, and the legal categories, in
themselves, may thus give a reasonable indication of differences
between offenders in the seriousness of their offences.

Secondly, details of the nature and extent of the offender's prior
criminal record were collected, as this was believed to be a prime
factor in determining the appropriate tariff sentence. Indeed, given
the limited jurisdiction of magistrates' courts to deal with serious
offences, it may often be a greater influence on the choice of
sentence than the number and nature of current offences. The
aspects of previous record examined were: the number of previous
court appearances resulting in a sentence; the nature of the most
serious previous offence; the nature of the most serious previous
offence in the last three years; the length of time at liberty from the
last court appearance to the date of the earliest current offence; the
types of sentences previously imposed upon the offender; and
whether or not at the time he committed the offence he was subject
to any non-custodial measures such as a suspended sentence, a
conditional discharge, or some form of statutory supervision.
Although this does not allow a completely comprehensive account
of the offender's previous criminal record, it is likely to approximate to the way in which courts appraise conviction sheets.

Thirdly, certain personal characteristics of the offender, which
the court would commonly consider and make allowance for in
selecting the sentence, were examined. This included, of course, an
analysis of age and sex, but it also comprised work record, present

employment situation, and the degree of family responsibilities, as indicators of what have loosely been called 'community ties'. The offender's occupational status was excluded because the information was not usually available, even to the court, in a way that enabled it to be usefully categorized—for example, according to the Registrar-General's social class index. A man described as an engineer could be anything from a professional civil engineer to a worker on an assembly line in a factory.

It might be argued that any comparison of offenders in relation to the sentence imposed on them, on the basis of this limited number of preselected characteristics, is futile, even from a tariff perspective, because circumstances vary with every case and it is impossible to take into account every factor germane to the sentencing decision. This argument is based upon a recognition of the fact that sentencing can never be a mechanical application of a body of principles to a set of facts, but rather involves consideration of a complex set of circumstances and offence and offender characteristics which might serve to aggravate or mitigate the seriousness of the offence—and consequently upon a belief that every case is unique and is treated as such. For example, Sparks criticized the methods used by Hood (1962) to investigate the sentencing practice of twelve magistrates' courts by arguing that he examined only 'a few of the many factors which might reasonably have been taken into account by the courts in his study', and that in any case what mattered was not the influence of each factor in isolation but their combination and the relative weights assigned to each (Sparks, 1965: p. 80).

However, three reasons can be presented to justify the comparison of only a limited number of characteristics. First, many other factors, although clearly relevant in some cases, are not easily collected or readily amenable to statistical analysis. Such factors include the offender's attitude in court, the degree of remorse he exhibits, and the influence, if any, of a plea for leniency by the offender or his counsel. Some particular aggravating or mitigating factor might also exist which strongly influences the court's assessment of the offender's culpability. On practical grounds it is simply not possible to take the influence of such factors into account in a meaningful way unless the actual court hearing is attended. Even then the assessment of their influence would be subjective and open to criticism.

Secondly, such factors are not consistently afforded as much weight as the more readily observable characteristics selected here, which are nearly always taken into account in sentencing an individual. Thus, despite their relevance, their influence on the choice of sentence is not likely to be strong enough to neutralize the descriptive potential of the observable factors.

Thirdly, as Hood has suggested, these other factors are not in any case customarily classified in such a way as to link them to the scale of penalties. Thus they may balance out between different cases, and in a comparison between different courts (Hood, 1962: pp. 14–15). For example, although the presentation of the circumstances and background of the offence and the offender in a social enquiry report may be framed, either deliberately or unconsciously, to evoke the sympathy of the magistrates, the actual response in terms of sentence may be far from predictable. The presence of a constellation of adverse factors in the offender's life may lead to his being given a 'chance' in the form of a more lenient sentence than he would otherwise have got, or conversely, it may lead to a stiffer penalty because of the magistrates' belief that, with such a background or life-style, the chances of rehabilitation are slight.

It is, of course, true that the conclusions drawn from the data on sentencing practice collected in this study rest upon unproven assumptions about the distribution of other considerations not taken into account and the relative weight that is attached to them in a tariff framework. However, a person making a decision of any sort will rarely be able to assimilate and take into account all the available information relevant to that decision, and some selection of material will therefore be inevitable. The selection is likely to be fairly narrow in magistrates' courts, where typically a large number of decisions are being made on the basis of a rapid and cursory examination of the information. If sentencers are making decisions according to any coherent policy at all, then in general they are likely to place the greatest weight upon the characteristics common to all cases.

The data were collected from police conviction sheets and social enquiry reports presented to the court at the time of sentence. For the most part these documents had been retained in the files of the Clerk to the Justices. However, the files were sometimes incomplete because, for example, the papers on a particular case had been removed as a result of an appeal against sentence and were not accessible, or because a copy of a report had not been kept on the file. When this occurred, the information was supplemented as far as possible by records held at county or local police headquarters or at the local probation office.

However, some of the material that would have been available to the court could not be traced for various reasons. Sometimes the conviction sheet had been sent by an outside police force, usually because the offender did not reside locally and had not been retained on local records; on other occasions a probationer had shifted residence to another county, necessitating the transfer of all his records to his new supervising officer. More often, certain items of information were genuinely missing, usually because a social enquiry report or an updated antecedent history had not been prepared. But the amount of inaccessible and missing data was never such as to jeopardize seriously the significance of the findings. In analysing differences between offenders on a whole range of characteristics, none of which has overriding significance, the occasional absence of one or two items of information is unlikely to upset the over-all picture.

There are of course limitations to the usefulness of data from official records, as they do not necessarily correspond to the information made available to the court. In some cases the court may have been given verbal information from the police or the probation officer which supplemented or contradicted the written documents, or it may have received information via a plea in mitigation by the defendant or his solicitor. Conversely, at times some of the information in the official police records may have been withheld from the bench. For example, the police may not have given the court details of previous offences which were regarded as 'stale', that is, as having happened too long ago to be of relevance to the present court appearance. Moreover, the extent to which a court is apprised of previous convictions for motoring offences, even serious ones, is a matter of some variation. Hood (1972) highlighted the debate that had been going on for many years about whether, in the case of a motoring offence, previous convictions for non-motoring indictable offences should be read out in open court or indeed made known to the court at all. Despite the fact that the Magistrates' Association in the past has pressed for the requirement that all previous convictions should be made known to the court so that it is in a position to decide which ones to take into account in passing sentence, such pleas as yet have been to no avail, and it is still left to the discretion of the relevant police force to decide what to disclose in a particular case.

There was no way of overcoming these limitations on the validity of the data. On the other hand, of course, official records do have the advantage of containing relatively 'hard' data, and therefore permit rather less subjectivity in coding and analysis than, say an assessment of the offender's attitude in court or of the extent to which a plea in mitigation is accepted.

Limitations of method

It is not possible for one research method to cover all aspects of the sentencing process in relation to the community service order. In particular, there are three important limitations upon the findings.

In the first place, no attempt is made to describe the use of the community service order in relation to every other sentence available to the court: in particular, the large number of cases dealt with by fine, discharge, or committal to the Crown Court for sentence were excluded. To have included even a random sample of cases fined or discharged would have more than doubled the time spent in data collection. In any case, the fine and discharge are used for a wide variety of indictable and non-indictable offences, often in situations where little information is available about the offender. Thus the data used to compare it with other sentences would have been more restricted and rather less meaningful. Similarly, information on cases committed for sentence to the Crown Court would often have been missing, as updated social enquiry reports are prepared at Crown Court level and files are forwarded on to the Crown Court by the Clerk to the Justices for the purposes of the later hearing. Neither could a comparison be made with offenders receiving Borstal training, as this sentence is not available to magistrates' courts.

Secondly, the study does not profess to draw firm conclusions about the 'displacement effect' of the community service order: that is, about the sentence that offenders given community service would have received before the scheme was introduced. This could properly have been investigated only by comparing a matched sample of offenders before and after the introduction of the scheme and observing differences in sentencing patterns. Even then there would have been problems caused by changing conditions with the passage of time and possible alterations in sentencing patterns independent of the introduction of the new measure.

The difficulties encountered in estimating the displacement effect of a new sentence are well illustrated by past studies which have attempted this. For example, Sparks (1971) and Oatham and Simon (1972) did retrospective analyses of the effect of the introduction of the suspended sentence by using the Home Office criminal statistics to indicate the proportionate use of each sentence available to courts before and after its introduction. Neither was able to give more than a rough estimate of how the use of the suspended sentence might have affected the prison population. Moreover, although methodologically similar, the studies came to different conclusions. Sparks held that it was probable that the suspended sentence had not reduced the numbers in prison at all, while Oatham and Simon tentatively estimated that there had been a saving in the prison population of between 850 and 1,900 by the end of 1970. Although Sparks presented more material to back up his conclusion, there is no decisive evidence that he was more likely to be right than Oatham and Simon.

In any case, the criminal statistics could not have been used for the same purpose in relation to the community service order because its gradual introduction throughout the country over several years would make a comparison from year to year of figures compiled on a national basis meaningless. In addition, other changes in the Criminal Justice Act 1972, such as those relating to the suspended sentence, may have altered the use not only of the suspended sentence itself, but also of other sentences such as imprisonment and the probation order, and to distinguish the independent effect of the community service order would not be possible.

The Home Office Research Unit attempted to infer the displacement effect of the community service order from a study of current sentencing practice (Pease *et al.*, 1977). The penal measures imposed upon three groups of offenders were considered: those sentenced for their original offences following a breach of one of the requirements of a community service order; those referred by courts for community service assessment but not given it; and those recommended for community service on the initiative of a probation officer but not receiving it. Also taken into account were probation officers' assessments in one county (Durham) of what the likely sentence would otherwise have been on those sentenced to community service. From this data the authors tentatively estimated that 45−50 per cent of those given a community service order were displaced from custody.

This estimate, however, is of questionable validity. First, as the authors admitted, custodial sentences may well be passed upon those who are in breach of a community service order not because such a sentence would originally have been imposed, but because the offender's failure to take advantage of the order is in itself seen as warranting a custodial sentence. Secondly, where the court asks for a community service order, but the court eventually imposes, say, a prison sentence instead, this may be because the case is considered, either by the probation officer or by the bench which subsequently imposes the sentence, too grave for a community service order. In other words, these are the cases in which it has explicitly been rejected as a substitute for imprisonment. The fact, therefore, that a prison sentence is eventually passed after a request for an assessment or a recommendation for the sentence is made, is no evidence that it is being used as an alternative to imprisonment. It can be used equally as well to infer the opposite. An assessment by probation officers of what the likely sentence would have been if a community service order had not been made, may provide a more reliable estimate of the displacement effect, but by itself it is hardly sufficient.

The difficulties inherent in any attempt to discover what effect a new sentence has on existing sentencing patterns are therefore clear. The present research was restricted to an examination of current sentencing practice *after* the introduction of the community service order. It could therefore provide a comparison between, for example, community service and imprisonment *only on the basis of the use of imprisonment at that time.* If offenders receiving a community service order differ significantly from those upon whom imprisonment is imposed, this does not necessarily mean that the community service order has not attracted offenders who, before the introduction of the scheme, would have received imprisonment. It may point rather to the possibility that imprisonment has been upgraded in the tariff as a result of the new measure. Of course, it has been possible to draw inferences about the displacement effect of the community service order from the nature of differences found between its use and the use of other sentences, but these inferences are merely tentative hypotheses raised in the light of current sentencing practice.

The third limitation is that no comprehensive investigation of the reasons for the imposition of particular sentences has been attempted. Many complex and overlapping factors influence the decision about the form of sentence and explain variations between sentencers and between courts. There are, for example, the legal constraints upon the exercise of judicial discretion; the sentencer's philosophy and views on penal objectives; the background and social class of the bench; the nature of the area in which the court is situated; and the personal characteristics, attitudes, and beliefs of those (such as probation officers and clerks to the justices) who advise sentencers. The structure of magistrates' courts further complicates the issues, as the bench is rarely composed of exactly the same three magistrates. Even the magistrates acting as chairmen of the bench vary a great deal; of the ninety-two selected sentences imposed in the first six months in Ipswich in this study, twenty-two different chairmen were involved. It is thus virtually impossible to assess the influence of a particular magistrate from a direct examination of sentencing practice. For these reasons, the data presented here do not offer the basis for a systematic analysis of what reasons enter into the determination of the sentence.

6

Variations in the use of the sentence

When a new penal measure first becomes available to the courts, there are two dangers, both springing from its novelty: first, that it will be underused because of ignorance, caution, or lack of enthusiasm on the part of sentencers; and secondly, that it will be overused and imposed in inappropriate circumstances because of excessive expectations of a new concept in the treatment of offenders. Both dangers are difficult to guard against, and it was clear from the outset that the community service order might be exposed as much to the second danger as to the first. It was also to be expected that courts would differ in the extent to which they would resort to the sentence, depending on the attitudes of the sentencers in each area to the scheme and the information which they had been given about it.

TABLE 1

The use of each selected sentence by each court

	Prison Sentences	Community Service Orders	Suspended Sentences	Probation Orders	Detention Centre Orders	Total
Ipswich	67	22	44	85	14	232
	28.9%	9.5%	19.0%	36.6%	6.0%	100%
Peterborough	31	32	47	90	3	203
	15.3%	15.8%	23.2%	44.3%	1.5%	100%
Nottingham	182	162	204	363	29	940
	19.3%	17.2%	21.7%	38.6%	3.2%	100%
Medway	44	58	64	75	11	252
	17.4%	23.1%	25.4%	29.8%	4.4%	100%
Bedford	41	13	51	69	9	183
	22.4%	7.1%	27.9%	37.7%	4.9%	100%
Cambridge	51	21	61	76	2	211
	24.2%	10.0%	28.9%	36.0%	0.9%	100%
Total	416	308	471	758	68	2021
	20.6%	15.2%	23.3%	37.5%	3.4%	100%

$\chi^2 = 71.4$ with 20 degrees of freedom; $p < .0001$

Marked variations occurred between the courts studied here in the use of all the sentences selected for comparison, as is illustrated in Table 1. These differences were highly significant.[1] For example, the rate of imprisonment at Ipswich was nearly twice that of Peterborough. And when the detention centre order was taken as a percentage of the sentences passed on offenders aged 17 to 20 (the only age group eligible for it) the rate at which it was used ranged from 4.2 per cent in Cambridge, 5 per cent in Peterborough, 18.8 per cent in Bedford, to 21.6 per cent in Ipswich. The least variation occurred in the extent to which the suspended sentence was used.

In individual comparisons of each court with every other court, it became apparent that the sentencing practices of Peterborough and Nottingham were fairly similar, as were those of Ipswich and Bedford. In all other comparisons, significant differences emerged in each case.

In particular, there were enormous variations in the extent to which the community service order was employed. Not surprisingly, Medway and Nottingham—the two courts in the pilot areas —had the largest proportions of orders, and in Medway the use of the sentence nearly paralleled that of the suspended sentence and the probation order. This was no doubt partly a reflection of the fact that their schemes had been in operation for over two years before the study of their sentencing practice commenced.

Nevertheless, the pattern of variations remained evident even when these two courts were excluded. Peterborough used the community service order more than twice as often as Bedford, and over 50 per cent more than Cambridge, even though the latter was situated in the same probation area. In some cases, the number of orders made fell considerably below initial expectations. For example, at the commencement of the study predictions of the likely number of orders that would be passed by a particular court were obtained from community service organizers, and the courts selected for investigation were chosen from those where at least twenty-five orders in a twelve-month period were forecast. In the event, it will be seen from Table 1 that the Ipswich, Bedford, and Cambridge courts all fell below this figure. In the case of Bedford, the number of orders passed was so small that it was difficult to draw any firm conclusions about the use of the sentence.

Some of the discrepancy in the use of the community service order might have been due to an initially cautious approach by those areas with schemes just commencing, especially ones with a smaller use of non-custodial measures. Much of the difference between Peterborough and Cambridge, for example, was due to the use of the sentence in the first six months of the scheme's operation.

In Peterborough seventeen orders were made during this period, as opposed to Cambridge's nine. Ipswich and Bedford were also more inclined than other courts to opt for community service orders of medium length, i.e. at least 100 hours but less than 180. In view of the problems reported by the pilot areas in the administration of very long orders, and the widespread belief that very short orders did not allow enough time for a therapeutic effect, this is scarcely surprising. Courts that lack confidence in the scheme might be expected to err on the side of caution in determining the appropriate length of an order.

There was some evidence that the use of the community service order tended to be inversely related to the use of imprisonment, that is, that a high use of one went with a low use of the other. Peterborough and Nottingham were distinguished by a comparatively low use of imprisonment and the detention centre order, while Ipswich and Bedford showed the reverse tendency. There was not quite such a marked division in the use of the probation order and the suspended sentence, but here too Peterborough and Nottingham had a slightly higher use of the probation order than Ipswich and Bedford, and a lower use of the suspended sentence than Bedford. In these respects, therefore, it appeared that Ipswich and Bedford were apparently severe, while Peterborough and Nottingham could be classified as apparently lenient.[2]

Evidence of apparent severity or leniency in sentencing practice was also derived from the action taken by courts for breach of a suspended sentence, probation order, or conditional discharge. Variations in the extent to which action was taken were extraordinary. The greatest fluctuation appeared in the rate of activation of suspended sentences. While Ipswich and Bedford sentenced offenders to all or part of the prison term originally suspended (*consecutive* to any prison term imposed for a new offence) in over 81 per cent of cases of breach, and in Medway 78 per cent, Peterborough did so in only 36 per cent of cases and Nottingham and Cambridge in less than 60 per cent. It was remarkable that three courts should have felt able to leave 40 per cent of suspended sentences unactivated on breach, in view of the statutory presumption in favour of activation 'unless the court is of the opinion that it would be unjust to do so in view of all the circumstances which have arisen since the suspended sentence was passed, including the facts of the subsequent offence' (s.23(1) Powers of Criminal Courts Act 1973). Moreover, the true rate of activation of suspended sentences in all cases sentenced in each court was no doubt lower than these figures reflect. The number of offenders excluded from the study because they were given a prison sentence for the new offence *concurrent* with the activated suspended sentence was very small. On the other hand, very many other cases involving breach of a suspended sentence were excluded because a fine or discharge was imposed for the new offence and no action was taken on the breach.

Ipswich and Bedford also imposed an additional sentence for the original offence far more often than any other court if a breach of a probation order had occurred, and were almost three times as likely to do so as Peterborough. Likewise, Ipswich sentenced for the original offence upon breach of a conditional discharge more than three times as often as Peterborough. Thus the description of the sentencing practice of Ipswich and Bedford as apparently severe and that of Peterborough and Nottingham as apparently lenient was reinforced.

The same unambiguous pattern did not emerge in the Medway and Cambridge courts. Although Medway made relatively low use of imprisonment and high use of the community service order, it also had a high use of the detention centre order and by far the lowest use of the probation order. On the other hand, while Cambridge resorted to imprisonment in a comparatively high proportion of cases and had a low use of the community service order, it also made less use of the detention centre order than any other court.

Despite these anomalies, it was nevertheless clear that the courts with an apparently severe sentencing practice, as reflected in their high use of custodial sentences, were less disposed to resort to the community service order than those with an apparently lenient sentencing practice.

It could be argued that a description of the proportionate use of the sentences selected for comparison here does not indicate the over-all severity or leniency of a court's sentencing practice, as the inclusion of fines, discharges, and committals for sentence might have presented quite a different picture. However, the conclusions reached here can be defended in two ways. First, the proportionate use of the selected sentences, as pointers to severity or leniency in sentencing practice, was confirmed by the action that each court took on the breach of non-custodial measures; it seems unlikely, therefore, that the inclusion of fines, discharges and committals for sentence would have upset the general trends. Secondly, the data do at least provide firm evidence of the frequency with which each court used the community service order in comparison with the other four selected sentences, which was the central purpose.

Local differences in offence and offender characteristics

Differences in the extent to which a sentence is used by different courts does not, of course, necessarily reflect *real* disparity in sentencing practice, as they might be due to differences between individual offenders. For example, a court with a comparatively high use of imprisonment might be sentencing offenders with more serious previous records than courts with a comparatively low use; or courts with a higher use of the detention centre order might be dealing with a greater number of young adult offenders. Real disparity only exists if differences cannot be related to any variations in the distribution of offence and offender characteristics relevant to the perspective from which sentences are being compared. Each court, therefore, was compared with every other court in the distribution of each selected characteristic to see how far any differences found *might* explain the apparent disparity in sentencing practice.[3] It emerged that there were, in fact, considerable variations in the distribution of the offence and offender characteristics considered relevant to a tariff sentencing structure. Out of 270 tables in which differences were tested for significance, 138 significant results were obtained, whereas only fourteen such results could have been expected purely by chance.[4] However, it was evident that, taken over all, the variations that did exist could only account for a small part of the apparent severity or leniency of the sentencing practice of individual courts. In many cases, too, the variations between the offenders dealt with by different courts actually appeared to increase rather than reduce the disparity in sentencing.

Turning first to the personal characteristics of the offenders themselves, the major difference in the distribution of the age of offenders occurred in the Medway court, which had a significantly larger proportion of young offenders, especially those aged 17 to 20, than Bedford, Nottingham, and Cambridge. For example, while only 22.7 per cent of the offenders dealt with by Cambridge were aged 17 to 20, 35.6 per cent of the Medway sample fell into this category.

This could account for three aspects of the sentencing disparity described earlier. First, it could account for the relatively high use of the detention centre order by Medway in comparison with Nottingham and Cambridge, as this sentence is only available to offenders aged 20 or under. Secondly, it could have been related to the high use of the community service order by Medway since, as Chapter 7 will show, this was reserved primarily for those aged 25 and under. Thirdly, in view of the statutory presumption against

Community service orders

the use of imprisonment for offenders aged 17 to 20,[5] it could account for the lower use of imprisonment by Medway in comparison with the Ipswich, Bedford, and Cambridge courts. This, however, was neutralized to some extent by the fact that Medway was more likely than any other court to use imprisonment for young adults (*infra*, p. 104).

There was also an unequal distribution of males and females among the courts, as demonstrated by Table 2. Peterborough,

TABLE 2
Distribution of males and females between the courts

	Male	Female	Total
Ipswich	194	38	232
	83.6%	16.4%	100%
Peterborough	154	49	203
	75.9%	24.1%	100%
Medway	221	31	252
	87.7%	12.3%	100%
Bedford	133	50	183
	72.7%	27.3%	100%
Nottingham	720	220	940
	76.6%	23.4%	100%
Cambridge	179	32	211
	84.8%	15.2%	100%

$\chi^2 = 27.98$ with 5 degrees of freedom
$p < .0001$

Bedford, and Nottingham all had a similar proportion of males and females, but all had a higher proportion of females than Ipswich, Medway, and Cambridge. Since there was a clear preference for the use of the probation order for females (*infra*, p. 105), this could have been the reason for some of the discrepancies in its use: the three courts sentencing a higher proportion of females all had a consistently higher use of the probation order than the other three courts, although the differences were sometimes even greater than would have been expected from the uneven distribution of females alone. Similarly, since there was an over-all reluctance by the courts to use imprisonment and the community service order for females, this might explain the differences in the use of these sentences between Ipswich and Cambridge on the one hand and Peterborough and Nottingham on the other.

Differences between courts in the community ties of offenders also corresponded to a small extent with variations in the use of sentences. Although the extent of family responsibilities was virtually independent of the distribution of males and females, the group of three courts which had a higher proportion of males—Ipswich, Medway, and Cambridge—also had fewer housewives and a greater number of offenders without any dependants. In Peterborough 14.9 per cent of offenders were classified as housewives, in Bedford 18.6 per cent and in Nottingham 17.9 per cent. In contrast, the proportion in Ipswich was 6.6 per cent, in Medway 9.7 per cent and in Cambridge only 3.3 per cent. On the assumption that greater domestic responsibilities invite a more lenient sentence, or at least a non-custodial rather than a custodial sentence, such differences can again partly provide an explanation for sentencing disparities.

The distribution of offenders between courts in respect of their employment situation and work habits were less easy to analyse. Many significant differences between courts did occur. However, many of these differences could be ascribed to the disparate proportions of housewives with which the courts were dealing. For example, the variations between Ipswich and Bedford, Nottingham and Cambridge, or Peterborough and Medway, were all attributable to this. Other differences on these variables, particularly in the dispersion of offenders who were *eligible* for employment (thus excluding housewives, students, pensioners, and the sick or disabled), were not consistently related to variations in sentencing patterns. At one extreme, Peterborough and Medway had the highest proportion of offenders who were employed and exhibited regular or fair work habits, while Nottingham and Cambridge had the lowest. For example, 55.6 per cent of the offenders in Peterborough who were eligible for employment were employed, in contrast with only 24.3 per cent in Cambridge; and 49.5 per cent of the offenders in Medway had regular or fair work habits, compared with only 29.2 per cent in Nottingham.

This might have contributed, therefore, to the high rate at which imprisonment was used by Cambridge, and to the low rate of its use by Peterborough. It might also explain Peterborough's tendency to use the probation order more often than other courts did. At the same time, it merely magnifies the apparent disparity between Nottingham on the one hand, and Ipswich, Medway, and Bedford on the other.

Differences between courts in the distribution of the personal characteristics of offenders could therefore be used to account for some of the variations in sentencing patterns. For instance, the high use of the detention centre order and the community service order by Medway might have been related to age and the low use of imprisonment by Peterborough and Nottingham could be partly attributed to the higher proportion of females dealt with by those courts. However, such differences were never large enough to explain more than a small amount of the disparity found. For example, differences in age were clearly not significant enough to account for the fact that Medway used the community service order more than twice as often as Ipswich, Bedford, and Cambridge; and differences in the use of the community service order between Ipswich, Bedford, and Cambridge on the one hand, and Peterborough and Nottingham on the other, remained completely unexplained. Similarly, while the distribution of males and females between courts was sometimes related to the use of imprisonment, this was not uniformly so: Bedford, labelled as a severe court for its high use of imprisonment, actually had the *highest* proportion of females, thus increasing the apparent disparity between that court and others.

Turning next to the previous criminal records of the offenders in each court, there were again a number of significant differences. These did little, however, to account for sentencing disparity, and in most cases they merely added to it.

This was so in the comparison between two of the apparently severe courts—Ipswich and Bedford—and two of the apparently lenient courts—Peterborough and Nottingham. The offenders in Peterborough differed significantly from those in Bedford on three dimensions: they were likely to have *more* previous court appearances, *more* previous fines, and slightly *more* previous custodial sentences. It is true that while Bedford had more offenders without prior custodial experience than did Peterborough, it also had more who had experienced at least eight sentences in the past. Nevertheless, it can be concluded that despite Peterborough's greater use of non-custodial sentences, its offenders clearly possessed lengthier and more serious criminal records than those of Bedford. The same pattern emerged in the comparison between Ipswich and Peterborough. There was only one significant difference—in the custodial measures to which the offenders had been subject as juveniles or young adults—and again this revealed a marked tendency for the Peterborough offenders to have more serious past records.

Even more pervasive differences were found between Ipswich and Bedford on the one hand and Nottingham on the other. The offenders sentenced in Nottingham had more former court appearances, on average, than those sentenced in Bedford; 45.7 per cent of the offenders in Nottingham had seven or more court appearances, in contrast with only 27.1 per cent of those in Bedford. More specifically, Nottingham was dealing with proportionately more offenders who were, or had been, subject to a suspended sentence, a community service order, or an attendance centre order; and its offenders had been subject, on average, to more custodial sentences. They had also had a shorter time at liberty since their most recent sentence, more fines, and more previous probation orders. Thus, on every variable where a significant difference was found, the offenders in Nottingham had more serious past records than those sentenced in Bedford.

The differences between Ipswich and Nottingham were in general smaller, but again they were without exception in the same direction. Offenders in Nottingham had had more former court appearances, slightly more fines, more probation orders, more custodial penalties, and more custodial measures as juveniles or young adults. They were also more likely to have already had a suspended sentence, community service order, attendance centre order, and discharge.

The differences in past records between the two apparently severe courts and the two apparently lenient ones were therefore the reverse of those which might have been expected if they were to account for the variations in sentencing patterns. Despite the lower use of imprisonment by Peterborough and Nottingham, and the higher use of the community service order and the probation order, the offenders sentenced there had consistently more extensive criminal records than those in Ipswich and Bedford. Thus, far from explaining the apparent disparity in sentencing, these differences increased it.

The comparison between the previous records of the offenders in Medway and those in every other court also disclosed several marked differences. Medway sentenced the highest proportion of offenders with no earlier court appearances, and the lowest proportion with fifteen or more. The differences from all other courts except Bedford were fairly substantial. Virtually every other significant difference between the offenders in Medway and those in the other courts was in this same direction. For example, the Medway offenders had, on average, fewer previous fines and probation orders than any other court. They also had fewer custodial penalties than the offenders in Nottingham and Cambridge. It is true that the offenders in Medway were also more likely than those in any other court except Nottingham to have been subject to a community service order or an attendance centre order in the past. However, this was no doubt due to the fact that the community service scheme had been operating in Medway for more than two years: it was noteworthy that fewer offenders in Medway had ever been subject to a suspended sentence than those in the other courts. The evident implication is that the criminal records of the offenders sentenced in Medway were likely to be consistently less extensive than those of the offenders sentenced elsewhere.

The differences between the records of the offenders in Medway on the one hand and those in Ipswich and Bedford on the other, although they were largely restricted to the number and type of previous non-custodial measures sustained, can therefore be used to account for the apparent disparities in sentencing between these three courts, especially when considered in conjunction with differences in age and sex. On the other hand, the fact that Medway sentenced offenders who possessed far less extensive past records than those in Peterborough and Nottingham means that its similarity with these two courts in the use of imprisonment and the community service order is misleading, masking a real discrepancy in sentencing practice. At the least, the inference must be that if imprisonment is the last resort in a tariff scale then those appearing in Peterborough and Nottingham were receiving it at a later point in their criminal careers than those being dealt with in Ipswich, Medway, and Bedford.

The differences between Cambridge and the other courts were more difficult to analyse. In comparison with Ipswich, Peterborough, and Nottingham, the differences in the number of former court appearances were somewhat equivocal. For example, while 12.3 per cent of the Cambridge offenders had no previous court appearances (a higher proportion than Ipswich, Peterborough, or Nottingham), at the other extreme 22.3 per cent had fifteen or more. But in comparison with those in Medway and Bedford, the offenders in Cambridge clearly had somewhat lengthier criminal records.

Cambridge was significantly different from Nottingham on every other aspect of former record except the number of fines. However, these differences were conflicting. On the one hand fewer offenders in Nottingham had been subject to a suspended sentence and fewer had eight or more previous custodial penalties; on the other, they tended to have experienced more probation orders and more custodial sentences as juveniles or young adults.

In comparison with the other four courts, the nature of the differences was less equivocal. Offenders in Cambridge had less experience of juvenile and young adult custodial measures than those in Peterborough or Medway; otherwise in respect of every significant difference they had more serious records. Cambridge sentenced a higher proportion of offenders who had already been given suspended sentences than any other court, and a higher proportion who had received a community service order or attendance centre order in the past than any other courts except Nottingham and Medway—which had community service schemes available in their areas during the experimental period. Of the offenders with five or more earlier custodial sentences, Cambridge had nearly twice as high a proportion as the other courts with the exception of Nottingham.

The interpretation is clear. Apart from Nottingham, the criminal records of those appearing in Cambridge were in general lengthier and more severe than those appearing in any other court. Moreover, the offenders in Cambridge tended to be polarized in terms of their criminal record, having fewer offenders in the middle categories and more at either extreme. Cambridge's higher imprisonment rate, at least in comparison with Peterborough, might therefore be explicable in terms of differences in past record, although again this has the effect of revealing a disparity between Cambridge and the severe courts—Ipswich, Medway, and Bedford.

The nature of the previous offences of which offenders in each court had been convicted confirmed these general trends.[6] Nottingham and Cambridge had a higher proportion of offenders who had committed offences of serious violence than any of the other courts (for example, 7.5 per cent and 8.1 per cent respectively against only 2.5 per cent in Ipswich), and a higher proportion with former offences of arson, burglary, or forgery (49.2 per cent and 50.8 per cent respectively against only 40.7 per cent in Ipswich). Conversely, Ipswich, Medway and Bedford all had a higher proportion than the other three courts of offenders whose most serious prior conviction was a motoring offence.

It is evident, then, that in terms of criminal record the six courts fell readily into two distinct groups. On the one hand, while Medway made less use of imprisonment and more use of the community service order than Ipswich or Bedford, its offenders had less serious criminal records. All three courts dealt with offenders whose earlier offences were significantly less extensive and important than those of Peterborough, Nottingham, and Cambridge. Such differences were largely the converse of those which might have provided an explanation of sentencing disparity.

Finally, some comment is needed on the nature of the offending with which each court was dealing. First, the most serious present offence in Nottingham was almost four times as likely as that in any other court to be a sexual offence. This was entirely due to the number of women—forty-five in all—who were convicted in Nottingham of loitering or soliciting for the purposes of prostitution. However, prostitutes did not necessarily receive a lenient disposal. A majority of them had already had convictions for the same offence and they were more likely than other females, with a comparable number of former court appearances, to receive imprisonment, a suspended sentence, or community service: four

(8.9 per cent) received imprisonment, seven (15.6 per cent) a community service order, nine (20 per cent) a suspended sentence, and twenty-five (55.6 per cent) a probation order. The high proportion of sexual offences was therefore inappropriate as a possible explanation of Nottingham's more lenient sentencing practice.

Secondly, Medway had a lower proportion of offenders convicted of burglary, forgery or arson, and a higher proportion convicted of offences relating to motor vehicles, than any other court. However, Medway did not treat the latter offences lightly. Of twenty-six sentences imposed for motoring offences, including driving while disqualified and drunken driving, six were imprisonment and fourteen a suspended sentence. And of twenty-four offences of taking and driving away, ten attracted a community service order, three imprisonment, three a detention centre order, and five a suspended sentence. The significance of this in terms of sentencing practice is difficult to evaluate. It may be that Medway dealt with these offences relatively severely because of a perceived need to impose deterrent sentences in that area, or it might be merely another reflection of Medway's generally harsher sentencing practice in comparison with Peterborough, Nottingham, and Cambridge.

Finally, Cambridge clearly sentenced a higher proportion of offenders convicted of public order offences than any other court. This was due principally to a group of middle-aged and elderly alcoholics, vagrants, and beggars who continually appeared on charges of public drunkenness, begging, and minor breaches of the peace. Of nineteen such cases in Cambridge, fifteen received a prison sentence of less than six months, and two a suspended sentence. This explains the high use (particularly of short terms) of imprisonment, by Cambridge. Again, it indicates that differences in the sentencing practice of Cambridge from that of Peterborough and Nottingham were explicable on a tariff basis, while in comparison the practice in Ipswich, Medway, and Bedford was far more severe.

Few differences emerged between courts in the number of offences of which the offender was convicted or which he asked to have taken into consideration. More offenders in Medway were convicted of only one offence than in any other court, and in comparison with Ipswich and Cambridge this reached significance (46.4 per cent against 32.3 per cent and 29.4 per cent respectively). More offenders in Bedford were convicted of only one or two offences than those appearing in Cambridge. A vast majority of offenders in all courts—between 73.3–80.3 per cent—had no offences taken into consideration. But the Medway sample had fewer offences taken into consideration than other courts, attaining significance in comparison with Peterborough and Cambridge. Again, therefore, it appears that the offenders in Medway could be classified as less serious, and the offenders in Cambridge more serious, than those in any other court.

In conclusion, then, most of the apparent inconsistencies in sentencing practice could not be attributed from a tariff perspective to local differences in offence and offender characteristics. For example, the distinctive features of the offenders in Medway might be used to explain the variations between that court and Ipswich and Bedford, but those same features increased disparities in the comparisons with Peterborough, Nottingham, and Cambridge. Likewise, the characteristics of the offenders in Cambridge might account for the difference in Cambridge's sentencing practice from that of Peterborough and Nottingham, but on the same basis would disclose inconsistencies in the comparisons with Ipswich, Medway, and Bedford.

Moreover, not all differences between courts went in the same direction. Peterborough sentenced proportionately more females and more offenders with family responsibilities, current employment, and regular or fair work habits, than Ipswich and Medway. This could explain some of the variations in sentencing practices between those courts, but not the disparity between Peterborough and Bedford. On the other hand, the offenders in Peterborough had more extensive and serious previous records than those in Ipswich, Medway, and Bedford. Similarly, although the offenders in Nottingham were more likely to be female and to have family responsibilities than those in Ipswich and Medway, their former records were far more extensive and serious, and they were less likely to be employed and to have regular or fair work habits.

Thus the sentencing practice of Nottingham and Cambridge, and to a lesser extent Peterborough, can be described as relatively lenient, while that of Ipswich, Medway, and Bedford can be described as relatively severe. In general, therefore, it is apparent that the severe courts were more reluctant to make use of the community service order. It is true that Medway in fact had the highest use while Cambridge had a relatively low use. However, this was probably due to the fact that the Medway court had been one of the pilot areas and therefore developed early confidence in the scheme for that reason,[7] and moreover that it was dealing with a greater proportion of young adult offenders; conversely, the offenders dealt with at Cambridge had certain unusual features which often made the community service order inappropriate for other than tariff reasons. For the rest, it appeared that courts with a preference for more severe penalties, particularly those involving custody, were less willing to make use of such an entirely new penal measure as the community service order than courts who already made liberal use of non-custodial measures. If this is an accurate indication of wider sentencing trends, then it is likely that any advice that the sentence be used as an alternative to custody is, to the extent that it is heeded, only preaching to the already converted.

7

The location of the community service order in the tariff

As a corollary of the fact that there were marked variations between courts in sentencing patterns, it follows that there were also variations in the types of offenders for whom particular sentences were used. But what were the nature of these variations? Were they differences in the relationship of sentences to each other (that is, their location in a tariff scale) or did they rather indicate differences in circumstances in which courts believed that a sentence at a particular point in a tariff scale was appropriate? For example, it would be possible for a sentence such as the community service order to be similarly placed in the tariff of each court, but nevertheless to be used for quite different offenders.

A description of the types of offenders for whom the community service order was used therefore required not only an analysis in each court of its tariff location but also a comparison between courts of the tariff scales which appeared to be in operation. A statistical comparison of the over-all characteristics of individual offenders and their offences was, of course, not easy and the inferences drawn from the data must be treated with some degree of caution as a result.

The method used was to compare offenders given each selected sentence in each court on every individual characteristic in turn, where necessary taking account of other relevant factors.[1] The statistics used (in this chapter *chi-square* (χ^2) and *phi* (ϕ)) are described in the Appendix.

Age

There was a highly significant relationship in every court between age and choice of sentence. The community service order was used predominantly as a sentence for the young offender. Less than 7 per cent of the community service cases were aged over 40 (compared with 15.3 per cent of the total sample), whereas 41 per cent were aged 17 to 20 (compared with only 24 per cent of the total sample).

This finding is consistent with the national figures for 1977. Of the 8,629 community service orders imposed throughout England and Wales by magistrates' courts, 4,443 (51.5 per cent) were given to offenders aged 17 to 20. In Crown Courts the proportion was similar: 1,611 (51.3 per cent) of a total of 3,139 (Home Office Criminal Statistics, 1977). It also accords with the experience of the pilot areas that operated community service schemes.[2]

This tendency to use the community service order predominantly for young adult offenders was less evident in Nottingham than elsewhere: only 29.6 per cent of offenders receiving it were aged 17 to 20. When offenders were split into those aged 25 and under and those aged 26 and over, only 57.4 per cent of offenders sentenced to a community service order in Nottingham fell into the lower age group, compared with proportions ranging from 77.3 per cent in Ipswich to 85.7 per cent in Cambridge.

When the offenders receiving a community service order were compared with those given imprisonment, a suspended sentence, and a probation order respectively, differences in age emerged in each case. The differences in this respect between the community service order on the one hand and imprisonment or the suspended sentence on the other were significant and substantial. In contrast, the differences from the probation order were smaller and reached significance in only two courts—Peterborough and Medway.

The fact that the total Medway sample contained a higher proportion of young adult offenders than any other court was not reflected in a greater use of the community service order for that age group in that court, except in comparison with Nottingham. Indeed, there was a strikingly high proportion of young adult offenders in Medway who received immediate imprisonment (eleven or 14 per cent compared with none in Bedford and only one in Cambridge).[3] Hence the difference between the community service order and imprisonment in respect of age was not significant and was smaller than that of any other court. When the effect of the number of previous court appearances was taken into account, this insignificant difference virtually disappeared.

In all other respects, however, differences in age could not be attributed to variations in the number of previous court appearances of the offenders. Thus age remained a highly significant discriminator between the community service order and other sentences (except, of course, the detention centre order, which is only available to offenders aged 20 or under).

This inclination to use the community service order for younger offenders is probably linked to the early belief that it was especially applicable as a rehabilitative measure to the young adult who was often lacking in a sense of social responsibility. It was thus interesting to find that, while the areas with schemes just commencing continued this emphasis, there were slight signs that the pilot areas —Nottingham and Medway—were adopting a broader approach, so that differences in age between the community service order and other sentences were less pronounced. This might reflect a belief that the initial emphasis was rather too restrictive, and that the community service order can have positive benefits—for example, as a means of developing a work habit—for a much wider age range. Nevertheless, at present the heavy concentration upon the younger age groups in the use of the sentence has generally been retained.

Sex

The community service order and imprisonment were both little used for females in any court, the vast majority receiving a probation order or to a lesser extent a suspended sentence. Of 416 prison sentences, only 26 were imposed on females; and of 308 community service orders, only 21 were imposed on females, 17 of these being in Nottingham. This could have been due to the fact that women had less serious previous records or that they were more likely than males to have dependants. However, this appeared not to be the case, as the differences remained unchanged when these factors were taken into account. For example, of those in the total sample with no previous convictions, 96.8 per cent of women received a probation order as against only 67.3 per cent of men. On the other hand, of those with seven or more previous court appearances, 28.6 per cent of females received imprisonment compared to 38.6 per cent of males.

This reluctance to use the community service order for females is again consistent with the experience of the pilot areas (Pease *et al.*, 1975: p. 29), and apparently is the practice in other areas with new schemes. In 1977, of a total of 11,768 orders made throughout England and Wales, only 660 (5.6 per cent) were imposed on females (Home Office Criminal Statistics, 1977). However, the fact that the community service order appears to be similar to imprisonment in this respect does not indicate that it was thought too severe a penalty for females. It was instead a result of the fact that women were more often perceived to be personally unsuitable for the scheme because of personal or domestic instability, pregnancy, dependent children, and so on. Thus it inevitably developed as a male-oriented sentence, regardless of its position in the tariff.

Community ties

Offenders receiving a community service order tended in every court to have stronger community ties than those receiving imprisonment, as measured by their family responsibilities, employment situation, and work habits. Although these differences were not always significant, they were often substantial. For example, of those offenders on whom information was available, in Nottingham 73 per cent of prison cases were single as against 54.9 per cent of community service cases, and in Cambridge 92 per cent as against 66.7 per cent. Similarly, in Cambridge only one (2.3 per cent) out of forty-three offenders who received imprisonment was employed and only three (10 per cent) out of thirty had regular or fair work habits; while, in contrast, six (30 per cent) out of twenty offenders receiving a community service order were employed and seven (36.8 per cent) out of nineteen had regular or fair work habits. The differences in the other courts, although less pronounced, were nevertheless in the same direction, and by and large remained unaffected by the number of previous court appearances.

This was a predictable finding. An indication of stability in at least one area of the offender's life was an important criterion in selecting him as suitable for community service in every area of this study, and the strength of community ties was in general the most effective measure of apparent stability.

A more surprising finding, therefore, was that the differences that emerged between the offenders receiving community service and those receiving a suspended sentence or a probation order all indicated that the latter had *stronger* community ties. For example, offenders receiving a suspended sentence were more likely to have spouses or dependants than those given community service, and apart from Peterborough this remained so after the age, sex, and number of previous court appearances of offenders had been taken into account. In Ipswich and Bedford this difference reached significance. There were also trends, which did not reach significance, for fewer offenders receiving a suspended sentence or a probation order to be employed and to have irregular work habits, although this was entirely due to the higher proportion of housewives given those sentences.[4]

Finally, nearly all offenders receiving a detention centre order were single, unemployed, and had irregular work habits. This was no doubt largely a result of the fact that they were all aged 17 to 20 and were therefore more likely than offenders given other sentences to be experiencing difficulties in employment.

In respect of community ties, then, there were more mitigating factors in favour of the offenders given community service than those given imprisonment, but fewer than for those given a suspended sentence or a probation order.

There were clearly some small differences between courts in the relationship of the community service order to other sentences. However, most of the variation between courts was not because of this, but rather a result of differences in the nature of offenders given all sentences. For example, the differences in family responsibilities and employment situation between offenders given a community service order and those receiving imprisonment were larger in Cambridge than in any other court. However, this was related to the fact that in Cambridge (of the offenders on whom information was obtained) only two out of forty-four sent to prison had spouses or dependants, and only one out of forty-three was employed. Thus Cambridge could at the same time have a greater proportion of community service cases who were single and a greater proportion who were unemployed than any other court.

Previous criminal record

In every court those upon whom a prison sentence was imposed were likely to have substantially lengthier criminal records than those receiving any other type of sentence. When offenders were split into those with up to four previous court appearances and those with five or more, the differences between the community service order and imprisonment were highly significant in each court except Peterborough and Bedford.[5] The differences were most pronounced in Ipswich, Medway, and Cambridge. In Ipswich 66.2 per cent of the offenders receiving imprisonment had seven or more previous court appearances, compared with only 22.7 per cent of the offenders given a community service order. The pattern was similar in Medway and Cambridge. In Peterborough, on the other hand, 79.9 per cent of prison cases had seven or more previous court appearances, compared with 50 per cent of community service cases.

There were thus some variations between courts in the relationship of the community service order to imprisonment. In two of the courts that appeared to have a lenient sentencing practice—Peterborough and Nottingham—the differences between offenders receiving imprisonment and those given a community service order were weaker than in any of the other courts.

Differences in the number of previous court appearances between those receiving a community service order and those given a suspended sentence were not significant in any court. There was, however, a slight trend in Ipswich, Peterborough, Medway, and Cambridge for offenders receiving a suspended sentence to have more extensive previous records. In Ipswich, for instance, although 11.6 per cent of the suspended sentence cases had no previous convictions, 48.8 per cent had seven or more, against only 22.7 per cent of those given a community service order.

In all courts there was a definite tendency for offenders receiving a probation order to have less extensive previous records than those given a community service order. The strength of the differences to some extent reflected the position of the community service order in relation to imprisonment. Because in Ipswich and Medway differences between imprisonment and the community service order were substantial, the differences between the community service order and the probation order were small and did not attain significance. On the other hand, the differences in Peterborough and Nottingham were larger and significant.[6] In Bedford there was also a clear difference,[7] although the numbers were too small to assess significance. Cambridge was an anomalous court. Although the difference between imprisonment and the community service order was similar to that found at Ipswich and Medway, nevertheless the offenders receiving a community service order had significantly more extensive previous records than those receiving a probation order.[8] This reflected the fact that Cambridge had a greater dispersion than any other court in the number of previous court appearances; it was thus easier to distinguish between the use of each sentence.

In conclusion, offenders receiving a community service order had less extensive previous records than those given imprisonment, and more extensive records than those receiving a probation order. There was also a small but insignificant trend in Ipswich, Peterborough, Medway, and Cambridge for the suspended sentence to be imposed upon offenders with more extensive criminal records than the community service order. Offenders sent to detention centres were in most courts spread throughout the range of previous court appearances. In Medway, however, six out of eleven had only one or two previous court appearances, while in Cambridge the two offenders who received this sentence had between seven and ten.

The question then arises: what aspects of previous record accounted for these differences? Were the differences linked mainly to custodial experience or rather to non-custodial experience? The answers to these questions might give some indication of the tariff location of the community service order. For example, the fact that offenders upon whom a community service order was imposed had significantly fewer previous court appearances than those receiving imprisonment does not *necessarily* demonstrate that the community service order was being used for some offenders who would not otherwise have been sent to prison. It might be that they had fewer previous court appearances because they had served fewer previous prison sentences. If so, this might indicate that the community service order was being used, at least, as an alternative to a first prison sentence.

Ten aspects of previous record were considered: the number of previous fines; the number of previous probation orders; the number of previous discharges or bindings over; the number of previous court appearances; whether or not the offender had been subject to a community service order, a suspended sentence or an attendance centre order; whether or not he had served a previous prison sentence; whether or not he had been subject to custodial sentences.as a juvenile or young adult, and if so, what they were; the length of time he had spent at liberty since his last court appearance; his most serious previous conviction; and his most serious previous conviction in the last three years. Combined scores measuring custodial experience and non-custodial experience were also devised as a check upon the comparison of the individual aspects of previous record.

In every court the community service order and imprisonment differed significantly in respect of both the offenders' custodial experience and their non-custodial experience. The differences were most pronounced in Medway and Cambridge. In Medway forty-four (75.9 per cent) of the offenders given a community service order had not had a previous prison sentence, compared with only fifteen (36.6 per cent) of those sent to prison. And whereas fifty-two (89.7 per cent) of the community service cases had no previous suspended sentence, this applied to only twenty (45.2 per cent) of the imprisonment cases. Similarly, in Cambridge fifteen (71.4 per cent) of the community service cases had never had a prison sentence, eighteen (85.7 per cent) had never experienced a suspended sentence, and ten (47.6 per cent) had had no more than one previous fine; the corresponding proportions for the offenders given imprisonment were 23.5 per cent, 31.4 per cent, and 15.7 per cent.

In Nottingham, on the other hand, the differences were less marked, although still clearly significant. Fifty-three (32.7 per cent) of the offenders given a community service order had no previous custodial sentence, as opposed to only twenty-five (14.9 per cent) of those given imprisonment. Likewise, only thirty-four (21 per cent) of the community service cases had three or more, as opposed to eighty-seven (51.7 per cent) of those who received imprisonment. There was a similar difference in the number of offenders who had been subject to a suspended sentence.

Notwithstanding these differences, it is noteworthy that in Nottingham seventy-two (44.5 per cent) of the offenders who received a community service order had two or more previous custodial sentences, a very high proportion in comparison with other courts. Moreover, the difference between the community service order and imprisonment in the offenders' experiences of custody as juveniles or young adults was in fact opposite to that which might have been expected: whereas 106 (62.4 per cent) of those receiving imprisonment had no previous institutional experience as juveniles or young adults, this applied to only seventy-six (46.9 per cent) of those given a community service order. One-third of the latter had a previous period of Borstal training, and thirty-four (21 per cent) had a previous detention centre order, as opposed to 22.9 per cent and 11.2 per cent respectively of those given imprisonment. The differences between these two sentences in the number of previous custodial sentences, then, resulted solely from differences in the number of previous prison sentences.

The differences between the community service order and the suspended sentence varied between courts. In Ipswich, Peterborough, Nottingham, and Cambridge, the offenders receiving a suspended sentence tended to have more previous custodial sentences and were significantly more likely to have served a sentence of imprisonment. Apart from that, their previous records were fairly similar to those of the offenders receiving a community service order. Thus it appeared that the suspended sentence was slightly more likely to be imposed upon the confirmed recidivist, but that in other respects its tariff position differed little on the criterion of previous record from that of the community service order.

In Medway, the offenders receiving a suspended sentence tended to have more extensive previous records on the non-custodial dimension: for example, they were likely to have more previous fines. On the other hand, the suspended sentence cases were likely to have had a significantly longer time at liberty since their last sentence than the community service cases. Thus, despite their slightly more serious previous records over-all, their immediate past tended to be freer of apparent involvement in crime.

In Bedford, the differences between the community service order and the suspended sentence, although small, were opposite to those encountered at any other court; that is, the community service order tended to be used for offenders with a *greater* number of fines and with *more* likelihood of a previous suspended sentence than those upon whom a suspended sentence was imposed. As in Medway, there was also a significant difference between the offenders with previous convictions in the length of time they had spent at liberty since their last sentence. While twenty-six out of the forty-six suspended sentence cases had lasted more than twelve months, only one community service case had managed to do so. Similarly, only half the offenders receiving a community service order had been at liberty for more than three months, as compared with over three-quarters of the offenders given a suspended sentence.

The differences between the community service order and the probation order also varied to some extent between courts. In three of the courts—Ipswich, Peterborough, and Medway—there was surprisingly little difference. In Ipswich and Peterborough, the community service order was as closely related to the probation order as it was to the suspended sentence. The only significant differences that emerged were in respect of the number of previous fines which offenders had received and their most serious previous convictions. While only one offender in Ipswich given a community service order had no previous fine, this applied to thirty-four of the eighty-five offenders receiving probation. Conversely, only fifteen (17.7 per cent) of the probation cases had three or more previous fines, as opposed to ten (45.5 per cent) of the community service cases. The most serious previous conviction of the probation cases was almost twice as likely to be theft, criminal damage, or a similar offence (e.g. obtaining by deception) as that of the community service cases (47.8 per cent as opposed to 27.3 per cent). In contrast, it was only half as likely to be an offence of violence, burglary, or forgery (30.4 per cent as opposed to 59.1 per cent).

In contrast, in Bedford, Nottingham, and Cambridge the differences between the offenders given the two sentences were significant and substantial in respect of both previous custodial experience and previous non-custodial experience. In Nottingham, there were significant differences on every aspect of previous record considered; nearly three times as many offenders given a probation order had no previous fine (32.7 per cent as opposed to 11.1 per cent), over twice as many had no previous probation order (50.7 per cent as opposed to 22.8 per cent), and over twice as many had no previous custodial experience (70 per cent as opposed to 32.7 per cent). There were similar differences in Bedford and Cambridge in respect of these three aspects of previous record. In all three courts, too, the most serious previous conviction of those with a criminal record also distinguished the community service order from the probation order. In Cambridge, while fifteen (78.9

per cent) of the offenders given a community service order had
been convicted of burglary and forgery, this applied to only fifteen
(28.3 per cent) of the offenders given a probation order. Conversely, the most serious previous conviction of twenty-three (43.4
per cent) of the latter was theft, criminal damage or a similar
offence, against only two (10.5 per cent) of those given a community service order.

The number of offenders given a detention centre order in each
court was too small to draw any firm conclusions about the
previous records of those given it. However, it was fairly clear that
there was little uniformity between courts in its use. In Ipswich the
fourteen offenders receiving a detention centre order clearly had
more minor previous records, on both the custodial and non-
custodial dimensions, than those receiving a community service
order. Only one had a previous custodial sentence, in the form of a
previous detention centre order. In Cambridge, on the other hand,
the two offenders receiving a detention centre order had both
previously received four or more fines, a probation order, a
discharge or binding over, and one institutional sentence. In one
case, the institutional sentence was a care order and in the other a
detention centre order.

In conclusion, the community service order tended to be used
more than imprisonment in every court for rather less serious
offenders in terms of previous record. The fact that offenders given
the community service order tended on the whole to have markedly
less extensive non-custodial as well as custodial experience than
those receiving imprisonment indicated that it might often have
been used as an alternative to sentences other than imprisonment.
On the other hand, in at least three of the courts it was clearly being
used for offenders with considerably more extensive and serious
previous records than those given a probation order.

There were clearly some variations between courts in the tariff
position of the community service order on this criterion. For
example, there was less difference between the community service
order and imprisonment in Nottingham than elsewhere. Indeed
there was a surprisingly high proportion of offenders with long
records of custodial and non-custodial sentences who were given a
community service order or a suspended sentence. Moreover, those
sentences were often imposed on second and subsequent occasions
when other courts would probably have resorted to custody. One
offender receiving a community service order in Nottingham had
had three such orders in the past (all successfully completed), and
another had had two as well as a suspended sentence in the past.
Likewise, one offender receiving a suspended sentence had

previously had a suspended sentence and three community service orders, and another a suspended sentence and two community service orders. It is thus plausible to suggest that, at least in respect of previous record, the community service order and the suspended sentence were being used more frequently than in any other court for offenders who would otherwise have been sent to prison.

Despite these variations, there was a surprising degree of consistency in the tariff position of the community service order. There was much more discrepancy in the circumstances under which a sentence at a particular point in the tariff was believed to be justified. The community service order occupied a fairly similar tariff position in Peterborough and Medway in respect of previous record. Yet, of the fifty-eight offenders receiving a community service order in Medway, eight had no previous convictions and nearly a third had only one or two previous court appearances; while, on the other hand, all offenders receiving a community service order in Peterborough had at least one previous court appearance, and only four (12.5 per cent) had less than three. It was also interesting to observe which aspects of previous record accounted for this difference. The previous custodial experience of the Medway offenders was likely to be just as extensive and serious as that of their Peterborough counterparts, and they were also just as likely to have had a previous suspended sentence or community service order. Where they differed was in the experience of fines, probation orders, discharges, and bindings over. Thus, in Medway 77.6 per cent of the community service cases had less than three previous fines, and 89.7 per cent had less than two previous probation orders, as opposed to 53.1 per cent and 65.6 per cent respectively in Peterborough.

Most of the previous sentences of the Medway offenders would probably have been imposed in the Medway area, and very often by the Medway Magistrates' Court. *Ex hypothesi*, the fact that, in comparison with other courts, the previous records of the offenders receiving each sentence in Medway were just as extensive and serious in respect of custody (or a threat of custody), but considerably less so in respect of most non-custodial measures, confirms that Medway was using imprisonment, the community service order, and the suspended sentence at a much earlier point in offenders' criminal careers than other courts.

The nature of current offending

Several difficulties confronted an assessment of differences between offenders in the nature and extent of their present offending. Only their most serious present offence could be taken into account, and there were inherent problems in constructing indices of seriousness.[9] Moreover, the grouping of offences for the purposes of comparison was to a small extent arbitrary, and resulted in the loss of much information. For these reasons, conclusions on differences between sentences on this dimension must be necessarily tentative.

The bulk of offenders (46 per cent) given the community service order in all courts were convicted, predictably, of property offences. However, this applied to every other sentence as well. Indeed, there was a surprisingly high proportion of community service orders imposed for offences of violence. For example, in Ipswich, Bedford, and Nottingham a higher proportion of offenders given a community service order were convicted of violence than of those given imprisonment, and only a slightly lower proportion than of those given a detention centre order. Offenders upon whom a community service order was imposed were also, in general, just as likely to have been convicted of burglary or forgery as those given imprisonment. In Nottingham 22 per cent of community service cases came into this category, as opposed to 14 per cent of prison and suspended sentence cases, and 13 per cent of probation cases. Peterborough was an exception to this: offenders receiving a community service order were less likely than offenders given either imprisonment or a suspended sentence to be convicted of violence, burglary, or forgery, and more likely to be convicted of theft, criminal damage, or a similar offence. In all courts except Cambridge the probation order was more likely to be imposed for theft, criminal damage, or a sexual offence, and less likely to be imposed for violence, burglary, or forgery than any of the other sentences.

Nottingham was the only court to use the community service order for sexual offences, imposing nine orders for soliciting or loitering for the purposes of prostitution. Few offenders received a community service order for drugs offences, but such offences were rare in any case. Indeed, it was interesting to find that of a total of six convictions on drugs charges in Peterborough, four resulted in a community service order.

It is probable that offences of violence (which were usually assaults occasioning actual bodily harm), burglary, and forgery, are usually perceived, *ceteris paribus*, to be just as serious as theft, criminal damage, public order, and motoring offences—and probably more so. On that assumption, it appears that the community service order was being imposed for offences that were at least as serious as those giving rise to imprisonment or a suspended sentence, and more serious than those resulting in a probation order. Sexual offences were the only definite exception to this; no community service order was imposed for a sexual offence other than prostitution.

The differences encountered between the community service order and other sentences in respect of the number of offences of which the offender was convicted, or which he asked to have taken into consideration, were slight and only reached significance in Nottingham. There were no differences in any court between offenders receiving a community service order and those given imprisonment in the number of offences of which they were convicted. In Nottingham and Cambridge, however, offenders given a community service order had more offences taken into consideration than those receiving imprisonment[10] and in Nottingham this attained significance.[11] There were trends in Peterborough, Bedford, and Nottingham for offenders given a community service order to be convicted of slightly more offences than those receiving a suspended sentence and in all courts except Ipswich and Cambridge there was a similar trend in comparison with those receiving probation. These trends did not reach significance.

One further aspect of the current offence pattern that distinguished the community service order from other sentences was those non-custodial measures that the offender had breached by committing an offence. As might have been expected, offenders receiving imprisonment in all courts were far more likely than those given a community service order to have been in breach of a suspended sentence. However, there were still variations between courts. In Ipswich, Medway, and Bedford, no community service order was imposed in a case involving a breach of a suspended sentence. On the other hand, in Peterborough four (12.5 per cent) of the community service orders were given to offenders in breach of a suspended sentence, in Nottingham thirteen (8 per cent) and in Cambridge two (9.5 per cent). These variations reflected the extent to which courts were willing to activate suspended sentences: thus offenders receiving a probation order in Peterborough, Nottingham, and Cambridge were also more likely to have been in breach of a suspended sentence than those in Ipswich, Medway, and Bedford.

The frequency with which the community service order was imposed when a breach of other non-custodial measures had occurred, varied markedly. In Peterborough, Bedford, Nottingham, and Cambridge, more offenders receiving a community service order had been subject, at the time of committing the offence or offences, to licence conditions following a custodial sentence, than those receiving imprisonment. In Peterborough two community service cases had been subject to Borstal licence and five to detention centre licence, a total of 21.9 per cent, as opposed to 6.5 per cent of prison cases. In contrast, in Ipswich no offender receiving a community service order had been on licence. It was evident, therefore, that the lenient courts and Bedford were willing to impose the community service order upon offenders who had recently been released from a custodial sentence, perhaps in the belief that it provided an opportunity for their reintegration with the community. Ipswich and Medway, on the other hand, were reluctant to use the community service order for such offenders. In all courts, the suspended sentence and the probation order were rarely used when a breach of licence had occurred, perhaps because the threat of custody would have been unlikely to act as a deterrent and supervision had already failed to prevent recidivism.

*   *   *

In summary, the use of the community service order in every court differed significantly from the use of both imprisonment and the probation order. Almost every difference between the community service order and imprisonment indicated that the former was often being used at a lower point in the tariff scale. The offenders receiving it were, on average, younger, had stronger community ties, and had less extensive experience of both custodial and non-custodial sentences than those sentenced to imprisonment. It is true that the principal present offence of the community service cases appeared likely to be at least as serious as that of the prison cases, and in all courts except Ipswich and Medway the community service cases were more likely to have been subject to licence conditions when committing one of the present offences. Nevertheless, the over-all tendency for the community service order to be imposed upon offenders who could be classified as significantly less serious (in terms of previous record and personal characteristics) than those receiving imprisonment was unmistakable. Conversely, apart from age, every difference between the community service order and the probation order indicated that the former tended to occupy a higher position in the tariff than the latter. There was a higher proportion of males among the community service cases, and on average they had more extensive experience of custodial and non-custodial sentences and comparatively serious present offences.

The differences between the community service order and the suspended sentence were more equivocal. Moreover, they were usually small and often not significant. In all courts the offenders receiving a community service order tended to be younger and, apart from Bedford, to have slightly less extensive previous records. In Bedford, however, they had slightly more experience of previous non-custodial sentences than those receiving the suspended sentence, and in Ipswich and Bedford they had somewhat weaker community ties.

Relative to other sentences, therefore, the community service order was generally located at roughly the same position within the tariff scale of each court. Most of the sentencing disparity reported in the previous chapter appeared to result from differences in the use of all sentences, so that the severe courts—Ipswich, Medway, and Bedford—resorted to custodial sentences at a much earlier point in offenders' criminal careers, and in far less serious cases, than the lenient courts—Peterborough, Nottingham, and Cambridge. Consequently the severe courts made earlier use of the community service order and the suspended sentence as well, and were less inclined to use the probation order in serious cases. Most of the offenders receiving a community service order in Peterborough, Nottingham, and Cambridge, therefore, would most probably have been imprisoned on a tariff basis in Ipswich, Medway, and Bedford.

There were, however, a few variations between courts in the relative tariff position of the community service order. For example, although the difference between the community service order and imprisonment in respect of community ties was larger in Nottingham than in any other court except Cambridge, the differences in respect of age and many aspects of previous record were much smaller, indicating that the community service order may have been located a little higher in the tariff scale than it was in other courts—especially Ipswich, Medway, and Cambridge. On the other hand, the difference between the community service order and the probation order, at least in respect of previous record, was larger in Nottingham and Cambridge than in any other court. It may be inferred that Nottingham was using the community service order rather more often in cases where imprisonment might have been expected as the appropriate tariff sentence in that court.

8

The policy of ambivalence

The foregoing description of the over-all relationship between the community service order and other sentences belies, of course, the range and diversity of offenders to whom it was applied. The use of the sentence can only be accurately described by outlining not only its over-all tariff location but also the diverse characteristics of individual offenders upon whom it was imposed. Thus it is important to consider the probable reasons why the community service order took the over-all tariff position it did, and to assess how far the stated objectives of the sentence were reflected in its use. First, how far was the initial ambiguity in the tariff location of the sentence evident in sentencing practice? Secondly, how did the potentially inconsistent objectives of the community service order affect its use as a tariff sentence? Thirdly, what practical features of the scheme modified or inhibited the application of tariff principles to the use of the sentence? In considering these three issues, particular attention has been paid to the operation of the scheme by the probation service and to the reasons given in social enquiry reports for recommendations in favour of a community service order, since no direct evidence was adduced to show what magistrates had in mind when imposing sentences.

The ambiguous location of the community service order in the tariff

As was shown in Chapter 2, the tariff position that the community service order was expected to occupy was never clarified when the sentence was introduced. The Wootton Committee felt unable to predict what use would be made of it. The Government, on the other hand, were committed to its use as an alternative to a custodial sentence, but on the grounds of political expediency did not want to exclude its use in other cases where existing non-custodial measures were deemed inappropriate or inadequate as a punishment, treatment, or deterrent. Thus the legislation did not include any provision analogous to the requirement inserted in the Criminal Justice Act 1972 that the court must decide that no other method than imprisonment is appropriate before imposing a suspended sentence. Instead, the community service order was merely restricted to offences 'punishable by imprisonment'.

Unfortunately, however, no clear consensus has emerged on the nature of the 'other cases' to which a community service order might properly be applied. The policy of encouraging the use of the sentence 'primarily but not exclusively' as an alternative to custody has been interpreted as a mandate for magistrates to impose it on any offender to whom they think it might, for varying reasons, be applicable. Bourke (1976), a stipendiary magistrate, has argued that the legislation specifically establishes the community service order merely as an addition to the existing range of non-custodial measures, which may sometimes be used as an alternative to custody but can also be used as an alternative to any other sentencing option available for the offence in question. Another magistrate (Johnson, 1976) has advocated that the expectation that the community service order should be used as an alternative to imprisonment should be removed as soon as possible; in his view shorter orders (i.e. 120 hours or less) fit naturally into the scale below the level of imprisonment.

There has been little guidance from higher courts on the types of offenders for whom it should be used. The Court of Appeal (Criminal Division) has considered the community service order on only a few occasions, either by way of appeal against a custodial sentence passed when a probation officer had recommended a community service order, or by way of an appeal against a sentence imposed for a breach of a community service order. On each occasion the Court has referred to the measure as an alternative to custody, but it is not entirely clear whether this is intended to be understood in a different sense than, say, a reference to the probation order or the fine as an alternative to custody. For example, in *R. v. Howard and Wade* (no. 3442/C/77), the Court stated:

> When a community service order is made, it saves the person in respect of whom it is made from an immediate custodial sentence. It is to that extent an indulgence to him, although it is hoped that it is also an advantage to the community if the order is complied with. If the order is not complied with, those who break the terms of the order cannot complain if a custodial sentence is imposed when they have thrown away the advantage which was offered to them.

As Thomas has pointed out ([1977] Crim. L.R. 638), this merely indicates that a custodial sentence is one of the available options when a breach of a community service order has occurred. It does little to clarify the location of the community service order in the tariff or the types of offenders for whom it might or might not be appropriate in the first instance.

A few probation areas have attempted to resolve the confusion by reaching an agreement with local sentencers about the use of the order. Nottingham, from the inception of the scheme in 1973, formulated a policy with the consent of local judges and magistrates, which proposed that it should be used only where a custodial sentence would otherwise have been imposed, or at least seriously contemplated. The final sentencing decision, of course, has remained with sentencers, and probation officers have assessed community service suitability whenever they have been requested to do so. Nevertheless, they have felt at liberty to draw the attention of magistrates to the 'alternative to custody' policy in circumstances where they have believed that a custodial sentence would not be merited by the court's sentencing practice.

All other areas in this study, however, relied upon the view that the community service order should be primarily but not exclusively an alternative to custody, and thus did not attempt to restrict it to any particular tariff bracket. The main reason for this was the belief that it should be made available as an individualized measure to any offender who might benefit from it. But two other factors were also mentioned.

First, there is the admittedly imprecise meaning of 'alternative to custody'. It necessitates a peculiar kind of mental gymnastics, since the court must determine that a custodial sentence would not be unreasonable on a tariff basis, but that the facts of the case make a non-custodial measure more desirable. This is complicated further by the fact that a new sentence that displaces offenders from custody may itself have the effect, in time, of altering opinions about the circumstances in which a custodial sentence is reasonable. After all, the probation order and the conditional discharge were both originally introduced as alternatives to custody.

Moreover, the probation order is still sometimes used for offenders who might have warranted a custodial sentence on a tariff basis. To that extent, even under an 'alternative to custody' policy, the community service order may be imposed upon offenders who would have received a probation order before the introduction of the scheme. Indeed, the Nottingham community service organizer recognized the possibility that the community service order may downgrade the probation order in the tariff as much as it may upgrade the prison sentence:

> Certain referrals of offenders by Courts for community service consideration appear to indicate the existence of one rather unfortunate effect to

the introduction of the Community Service Order, upon the status of the probation order. At times it has been implicit if not explicit that Courts see Community Service as a more appropriate alternative to a custodial sentence, than a probation order. . . . While it is recognized that the gravity of the offence is a factor here, nevertheless it would be unfortunate if the extensive experience of the probation service and its increasing involvement in the supervision of the more serious adult offender were to be devalued by a single addition to the range of methods it can command. (Nottinghamshire Probation and After-care Service, 1975: p. 26)

More importantly, an 'alternative to custody' policy has sometimes been rejected because it requires a probation officer, before making a community service recommendation on his own initiative, to predict whether or not the court will regard a custodial sentence as reasonable. It might be argued, of course, that it is not the task of the probation officer to anticipate the court's view of the case. However, this ignores the vital influence of the probation service in the sentencing process, especially in the selection of offenders for community service. Whether he likes it or not, the probation officer must attempt to anticipate the court's view of the case. But how can the probation officer assess whether or not it is reasonable to anticipate a custodial sentence? Should he think in terms of the most severe penalty which the most severe bench in that court would impose, or only the average penalty which the average bench would impose? Should he make a firm recommendation for a community service order only if he knows the full details of the offence or offences with which the offender is charged?

Probation officers in Nottingham often overcame this problem by adding to a community service recommendation the rider, 'if the court should be considering a custodial sentence'. However, this rider appeared to become a ritual, which avoided the necessity for probation officers to consider whether a custodial sentence would be reasonable and encouraged courts to subvert the 'alternative to custody' policy. Other areas preferred not to operate such a rigid policy. The organizer in Kent (Medway), for instance, stated after the first year of the scheme's operation:

In the early stages of the experiment, many probation officers felt that they must anticipate when the court was likely to make a custodial sentence. The reality of the situation is, of course, that a probation officer cannot presuppose the court's decision and can only provide professional advice in the light of information gained whilst pursuing a social inquiry report. During the last 12 months, I have constantly advised officers to use community service as a sentence in its own right for offenders who *could* go to prison. (Sussex, 1974: p. 6)

Community service orders

Table 3 sets out the reasons presented for community service recommendations made on the probation officer's own initiative. It is clear that whatever the area's expressed policy the use of the sentence as an alternative to custody was mentioned in a substantial proportion of such recommendations in all courts. But, as was

TABLE 3

Reasons for recommendations for community service orders

	Ipswich	Peterborough	Medway	Bedford	Nottingham	Cambridge
As an alternative to custody	6 50.0%	11 47.8%	12 42.9%	4 50.0%	54 58.7%	8 61.5%
As an alternative to other non-custodial measures	2 16.6%	0	4 14.3%	0	8 8.7%	2 15.4%
To benefit the offender	2 16.6%	9 39.1%	4 14.3%	6 75.0%	57 62.0%	3 23.1%
To benefit the community	2 16.6%	5 21.7%	0	4 50.0%	10 10.9%	1 7.7%
Other reasons (reparation, expiation, retribution, deterrence)	3 25.0%	2 8.7%	3 10.7%	2 25.0%	3 3.3%	2 15.4%
No specific reason	2 16.6%	2 8.7%	2 7.1%	2 25.0%	10 10.9%	2 15.4%
Total number of cases	12	23	28	8	92	13

N.B. Percentages do not total 100% because more than one reason was often given for one recommendation.

suggested earlier, the probation officer's reasons did not necessarily conform with his area's policy. In four courts, including Nottingham, a community service order was recommended in a small proportion of cases specifically as an alternative to other non-custodial measures. It is interesting to compare this with the finding of the Home Office Research Unit that 'by and large officers' views of community service in the range of sentencing alternatives did not correspond very closely to their area's expressed view' (Pease *et al.*, 1975: p. 55).

There were numerous individual illustrations of the obvious lack of consensus on the proper tariff position of the community service order, and its widely varying uses from a tariff perspective. Some offenders receiving a community service order clearly had previous records and present offences which were as serious as most of those given imprisonment:

> In Ipswich, an offender convicted of four offences, including burglary, was sentenced to 160 hours community service. He had over ten previous convictions, and had received two previous prison sentences and two previous detention centre orders. In addition, he had previously been subject to a suspended sentence, an attendance centre order and numerous fines and probation orders. The community service organizer had some hesitation in accepting him as suitable for community service work.

> In Peterborough, an offender convicted of several offences, including forgery and several theft counts, was sentenced to 175 hours community service. In addition, he had thirty-two offences taken into consideration. He had at least seven previous convictions, including one of robbery, and he had served three previous custodial sentences, including one prison term of more than twelve months. At the time of the current offences, he was already subject to a suspended sentence.

> In Nottingham, an offender was convicted of one offence of burglary and given 240 hours community service whilst still subject to parole, having been released from prison three months earlier. Apart from the full range of non-custodial measures, including a suspended sentence, he had previously received seven custodial sentences. He was a drug addict, who had come off heroin during his most recent prison sentence. (Interestingly, this offender completed his order in spectacular fashion (although needing treatment in an addiction unit), and a year later was working in full-time employment with the voluntary agency with which he had been placed. The case illustrates the risks and the potential benefits of imposing community service orders upon selected drug addicts.)

> Again in Nottingham, an offender was sentenced to 150 hours community service for two offences of burglary and arson. He had more than twenty previous convictions, and had served three custodial sentences, one of Borstal training and two of imprisonment. The offences had been committed within three months of his last court appearance.

> In Medway, an offender was convicted of one offence of theft and given 100 hours of community service. He had over ten previous convictions, and had served five previous custodial sentences, including Borstal training and imprisonment. He had also been subject to a probation order, an attendance centre order and numerous previous fines.

> In Bedford, an offender subject to Borstal licence was convicted of inflicting grievous bodily harm and sentenced to 100 hours of community service. His six previous offences displayed a distinctive pattern of

violence, thus giving rise to some doubts about his suitability for community service.

In Cambridge, an offender convicted of two offences involving theft was sentenced to 120 hours community service. He had twenty-eight previous court appearances, at which he had received four custodial sentences (including one prison term of more than eighteen months), two probation orders, and many fines and discharges. At the time of the offence he was already subject to a suspended sentence.

In some of these cases, the community service order served to interrupt a succession of institutional sentences; for others, it probably operated to postpone the point at which a first prison sentence became inevitable.

But there were also many examples of the community service order being used for trivial offences and for offenders with minor criminal records: cases where imprisonment would have been highly unlikely. These examples demonstrated not only the failure by probation officers and courts to follow an 'alternative to custody' policy but also a lack of clarity in defining the sentences which, for the purpose of such a policy, should be regarded as 'custodial'.

First, a detention centre order, for not less than three months and in certain circumstances up to six months, is available to magistrates' courts for offenders aged under 21. Since a community service order was believed to be especially appropriate for young adult offenders, it was natural that detention centre orders should often have been included among the custodial sentences to which it could properly be used as an alternative. This had important consequences for the location of the community service order in the tariff, at least for that age group. Considerable ambiguity surrounds the use of the detention centre order: on the one hand it may be used as a penalty for young offenders with a long history of offending, and on the other it may be imposed as a 'short sharp shock' or a treatment for novices in crime who might be taught respect for the law by the detention centre regime. The most recent official report on detention centres, by the Advisory Council on the Penal System, stated:

> We recognize that some offenders with long records of previous convictions have confined themselves to relatively trivial offences; and it is understandable that in such cases the courts should several times try the effectiveness of non-custodial methods before resorting to a detention centre order. The range of non-custodial treatment is at present limited, however, and it seems to us that if detention in a detention centre is to be effective it is to be applied before the young offender has achieved a

long string of previous convictions. . . . In general . . . *it is those with few previous convictions or none who are most likely to benefit from detention in a detention centre* [my emphasis]. (Home Office, 1970c: para. 129)

This ambiguity appeared to be reflected in the use of the detention centre order in the courts studied here. Only in Cambridge was it uniformly applied to serious offenders and offenders with several previous convictions. Its use in other courts for more minor offences greatly widened the scope for the use of the community service order for offenders aged 17 to 20 without departing from the idea that it was an alternative to custody:

> In Ipswich, two cases which had been adjourned for a social enquiry report with a warning that a detention centre order was being considered, resulted in a recommendation, which was followed, in favour of a community service order as an alternative. Both offenders had only one previous conviction, and in one case this had been incurred more than three years earlier as a juvenile. Both had two present offences involving property worth no more than £25, and no offences taken into consideration. Imprisonment would have been highly unlikely; detention centre was a distinct possibility.

In the case of many other offenders receiving a community service order, although detention centre was not specifically mentioned, it was obviously an option which the court might have considered, thus justifying the recommendation and imposition of a community service order as an alternative:

> In Bedford, a youth convicted of one offence of burglary, in conjunction with other more criminally sophisticated youths, received a community service order of 120 hours. He had no previous convictions apart from a minor motoring offence, and although he was unemployed he had a good work record and was reported to come from a good home. The community service organizer felt that this was a case where a detention centre order might have been considered, although imprisonment would clearly have been inappropriate.

The consequence was that the community service order was freely available, even as an alternative to custody, for almost any offender aged 17 to 20 convicted of an imprisonable offence.

Secondly, the suspended sentence is sometimes regarded as a custodial sentence, despite the fact that it often remains unactivated after the commission of a further offence. For example, the Home Office Research Unit found that, of 179 probation officers who completed a questionnaire in all of the community service experimental areas except Inner London, 78 regarded a suspended sentence as custodial, while 89 viewed it as non-custodial; the other

12 giving no indication either way (Pease *et al.*, 1975: p. 55). The view taken appeared to be linked with the officers' opinions of the relationship of the community service order to other disposals. If they regarded the suspended sentence as non-custodial, they were more likely to consider the community service order to be available as an alternative to non-custodial as well as custodial sentences: 74 per cent of them took this view, as against only 54 per cent of those who regarded the suspended sentence as custodial. It was thus significant to find, as described in Chapter 7, that the differences between the suspended sentence and the community service order were small and sometimes ambiguous. To the extent that the suspended sentence was used for a wide range of offenders, its definition as a custodial sentence allowed considerable latitude in the use of the community service order as an alternative to custody.

Apart from this obscurity in the definition of custodial senten-ces, many community service orders were recommended and imposed in circumstances where a custodial sentence was apparently not anticipated by a probation officer. Some of these were recommended for the purposes of rehabilitation, others were thought appropriate merely because other non-custodial measures were considered unsuitable, for example, because the offender's financial situation precluded a fine or because probation was unnecessary or unlikely to be effective:

> In Ipswich, two male offenders, aged between 21 and 25, each received a community service order of 120 hours for an offence of theft of property valued at no more than £25. Each had one previous conviction for a property offence, for which he had been fined. In one case the probation officer supported the suggestion of a community service order on the basis that a probation order would serve no useful purpose.

> In Medway, a probation officer recommended a community service order (which was subsequently imposed) on the grounds that the defen-dant 'is not at present in a position to pay a fine and *as a first offender is not to be recommended for a custodial sentence*' [my emphasis]. On another occasion, an offender with no previous convictions, who was described by the probation officer as 'essentially a hard-working and responsible family man', was given a community service order of 130 hours for one offence of handling stolen goods worth no more than £50.

> In Cambridge, an offender aged between 21 and 25, who had no previous convictions, was given a community service order of 180 hours for three offences, the most serious of which was burglary. He was employed and had a reasonable work record. The probation officer, recommending a community service order on his own initiative, stated, 'X is adamant that he does not want a probation order. He is, however, anxious to make reparation for his actions by means of undertaking a period of community work, since he has no money with which to pay a fine.'

It is not possible to prove that imprisonment or a suspended sentence was not being considered in these examples. However, imprisonment, at least, would have been highly unlikely. Even Medway, demonstrably the court with the most severe sentencing practice, imposed imprisonment upon only two offenders with no previous convictions. One was convicted of two offences of assault occasioning actual bodily harm and the other of offences under the Firearms Act; and both sentencing decisions were reversed on appeal. In general, then, it was clear that the ambiguous location of the community service order in the tariff was reflected in the sentencing practice of the courts studied here.

The general lack of consensus was also reflected in different views about the appropriate number of hours to impose. Despite reliance upon the policy that the community service order was primarily but not exclusively an alternative to custody, some areas nevertheless attempted at the beginning of the scheme to suggest a tariff scale roughly comparable to custodial sentences of different lengths, to act as an approximate guide to courts in selecting the number of hours. Cambridge suggested to sentencers that 120 hours should be regarded as roughly equivalent to six months' imprisonment and 240 hours as comparable to twelve months' imprisonment. This tariff was even cited in open court on at least one occasion (*Cambridge Evening News*, 10/4/76). In Bedford, on the other hand, a letter was circulated to sentencers and justices' clerks before the commencement of the scheme, suggesting that orders of up to eighty hours should be treated as equivalent to detention centre or up to six months' imprisonment, orders from 80 to 120 hours as equivalent to Borstal training or up to twelve months' imprisonment, and orders over 120 hours as equivalent to over twelve months' imprisonment. The effect of such varying guidelines upon sentencing practice was difficult to gauge, but it was further evidence of the ambiguity surrounding the use of the sentence.

The conflicting objectives of the community service order

It has already been demonstrated that, although the objectives of the community service order have been expanded and made more explicit since the introduction of the scheme, the potential conflict between them has never been fully admitted, let alone resolved; thus the initial deliberate ambivalence has been perpetuated. Such ambivalence is not, of course, peculiar to the community service order; the attempted fusion of tariff and individualized considerations has been characteristic of many other penal measures, including imprisonment, for much of this century. But these other measures have increasingly been weighted towards one set of considerations or the other. The community service order, on the other hand, has vacillated between the requirements of the tariff and the hopes of meeting individual needs.

As has been pointed out, this was the main reason for the rejection of the 'alternative to custody' policy in some areas. Many probation officers were unwilling to sanction a policy that might exclude the use of the community service order on tariff grounds in circumstances where it appeared particularly suitable as a treatment, although at the same time they did not wish its value as an alternative to custody to be undermined. A N.A.P.O. Working Party, for example, stated:

> We considered as a question of basic philosophy whether CSOs should be made exclusively as alternatives to custodial sentences, or whether they should be considered as sentences in their own right: we note the even division of opinion in this matter in the pilot areas. In our opinion it is proper to regard CS as a sentence in its own right, though we certainly hope that an important result of its general introduction will be a large reduction in the prison population. We do not see that it is possible to impose serious consideration of a custodial sentence as a prerequisite to a CS order, neither do we see why, given the positive treatment potentialities of CS, less serious offenders should be deprived of the opportunity of a form of disposal which may be particularly suited to their need. (National Association of Probation Officers, 1975: p. 1)

In a similar vein, the Durham community service organizer declared:

> The community service order should be deemed an alternative sentence and not exclusively an alternative to a custodial sentence. . . . In the CS team we are conscious of the rising prison population, and as CSOs have a role to play as alternatives to custodial sentences we urge that Courts make as many orders as possible, in appropriate cases, to curtail the number of prison sentences being passed. At the same time, we would not wish that an individual be deprived of the benefit of an Order because he does not fit the category of potential prison candidate. (Durham Probation and After-care Service, 1977: p. 6)

These statements ignore the inevitable incompatibility between tariff and individualized considerations in particular cases, and assume that some reconciliation of objectives can be achieved.

Of the areas in this study, only Nottingham as a matter of policy gave precedence to tariff requirements and insisted on the use of the sentence only as an alternative to custody; but even then this policy was not always followed by field probation officers when making recommendations. Organizers in other areas were aware of a possible conflict between tariff and individualized considerations, but nevertheless wished to take full advantage of the rehabilitative possibilities of the sentence. Whether or not the circumstances of the case merited a community service order on a tariff basis became just one of many selection criteria; other positive features in favour of a community service order, including its suitability as a treatment measure, could legitimately outweigh the fact that it might not be justified by tariff considerations.

Illustrations could be found in every court of community service orders that were recommended on rehabilitative grounds (and subsequently imposed) despite the perceived improbability that a custodial sentence would have been under consideration. The following are a few examples:

> In Bedford, a woman aged between 17 and 20, with no previous convictions, received a community service order of 100 hours (and a fine) for two offences of theft involving property worth no more than £25. The order was imposed on the initiative of the probation officer. The community service organizer's report to the Court stated that the offender had experienced no sense of achievement and was losing motivation, and thus could benefit from the experience of giving service to others. It went on 'Although such an order was introduced primarily as an alternative to custody, it can also be used for any other case where the offender is considered suitable.'

> In Nottingham, an offender aged between 17 and 20, with two previous convictions, received a community service order for 120 hours for three offences of theft. The social enquiry report stated that a fine would do little to lift him from his present lethargy, while he lacked sufficient motivation for a short period of probation. It continued, 'Although I am reluctant to suggest a community service order where a custodial sentence may not be under serious consideration, I feel in this case it would be appropriate in requiring him to do something which he might come to feel is satisfying and worthwhile.'

> In Peterborough, a male offender, with one previous conviction for which he had received a conditional discharge more than three years earlier, received a community service order for sixty hours for two offences of theft, involving property worth not more than £25. The probation officer suggested 'that the present offences were contrary to his previous behaviour but that there is perhaps some risk of him drifting into further offences if his undoubted abilities are not put to positive use'.

The ambiguity in the objectives of the community service order was therefore the primary reason for probation officers' unwillingness to accept tariff restrictions upon its use. That unwillingness appeared, in turn, to encourage courts to use it for the less serious offender.

The conflict that arose from this ambiguity was also reflected in the number of hours that were thought appropriate in particular cases. The willingness of probation officers to recommend an appropriate length or range of hours varied widely between courts. While at one extreme the probation officers in Peterborough recommended a specific length of order in over one-third of cases, at the other extreme those officers in Medway and Cambridge made no mention of length in over 95 per cent of cases. Moreover, while the one recommendation made in Medway and Cambridge respectively was not followed in either case, in Ipswich seven out of eight recommendations were followed, in Peterborough ten out of fifteen, and in Nottingham forty-five out of sixty. The point of conflict emerged in the reasons that supported recommendations of length. In Ipswich and Cambridge no such reasons were given. Of the fifteen recommendations in Peterborough, thirteen were without supporting reasons, while the remaining two invoked the offender's treatment needs. In Nottingham, on the other hand, while twenty-five recommendations were without supporting reasons, twenty-seven mentioned practical limitations arising from the offender's personal circumstances, five were made because of 'the nature of the offence', and only three were made on treatment grounds. In Bedford, too, one recommendation was based upon the nature of the offence, the other upon practical considerations.

There was thus little uniformity in the extent to which recommendations on length were made, the extent to which they were followed, or the reasons given for them. Apart from variations in the tariff used as a guide for determining the length of orders, there was no consensus on the other criteria which should properly be taken into account. The potential incompatibility between tariff and individualized considerations emerged most clearly when a probation officer advocated a medium- or long-term order, regardless of tariff requirements, because in his view the offender would benefit most from an order of that length. For example:

> In Nottingham, a probation officer, while admitting that a custodial sentence might not be under serious consideration, nevertheless recommended an order in the region of 100 to 120 hours 'in order to sustain [the offender's] interest while being long enough to get him fully involved'.

Practical modifications of tariff principles

Apart from the deliberate ambiguity in the tariff location and the objectives of the sentence that has been fostered by the probation service, a number of practical factors in the selection of offenders for community service clearly modified the extent to which it was able to serve as an alternative to custody. The success of the community service scheme is dependent upon community co-operation and goodwill; organizers could not expose the work-providing agencies to an intolerably high risk, either of reoffending or of chronic absenteeism. Normal tariff considerations, therefore, were not sufficient to determine whether an order was appropriate: selection was necessarily limited by criteria of personal suitability. The organizer's power of veto (*supra*, p. 32) enabled offenders for whom a suitable work placement could not be found to be excluded.

There was, of course, a temptation for probation officers to recommend the application of every available non-custodial measure before the court finally resorted to imprisonment, and the Ipswich organizer hoped that in time no offender would need to be excluded on grounds of personal unsuitability. However, this was clearly unrealistic, at least given the current methods of implementing orders. Despite the recognized difficulty of predicting whether offenders would be a success or failure on community service, readily identifiable and commonly accepted criteria certainly existed at the time of this study for distinguishing offenders who presented an unacceptable risk.

The four areas with schemes just commencing were clearly more cautious and stringent in selecting offenders than Medway and Nottingham. In the early days of the scheme in Ipswich and Peterborough, for example, probation officers were directed to ask seven specific questions as a guide to their assessment of community service suitability:

Is the offender likely to get a non-custodial sentence?
Is there a need for casework?
Are there medical problems?
Does the person have unusual working hours?
Does the person have a history of violent or sexual offences?
Does the person have active leisure interests?

If five or more of these questions were answered in the negative, then the probation officer should regard the offender as *prima facie* eligible for community service. No such rigid guidelines existed in Medway and Nottingham, and before long they were of little practical significance in the areas with new schemes.

However, there were nine personal characteristics which in every area were agreed to put an offender's suitability for community service in doubt:

1.   the absence of a settled home address or some other area of stability such as work or family commitments;

2. strong addiction to drugs or alcohol;
3. offending which involved serious or habitual violence or sexual aberration: as the Bedford community service organizer stated, while the scheme depends heavily on involvement with voluntary organizations, 'risks of violence, however "calculated" they may be, cannot be justified';
4. total lack of motivation to carry out the order (although motivation might merely stem from the offender's desire to avoid a custodial sentence);
5. domestic or work commitments that appeared likely to interfere with the offender's ability to perform an order within twelve months;
6. evidence of mental illness or severe mental disturbance;
7. a physical handicap which could not be accommodated within the available work placements;
8. the existence of problems which, in the probation officer's judgement, indicated a need for long-term casework;
9. unreliability on reporting during a previous period of probation.

It was also stated in Nottingham that experience had indicated that offenders who were part of a predominantly antisocial culture were likely to be unsuitable candidates for community service (Nottinghamshire Probation and After-care service, 1975: p. 9).

None of these factors automatically precluded consideration of a community service order. Relative unsuitability in one area could always be compensated for by other favourable characteristics. All organizers insisted that the constellation of factors in each individual case should be considered on its own merits. For example, although alcoholics or drug addicts were usually unsuitable, some sign of increased stability in their lives or a desire to change might indicate otherwise. Moreover, although only one offender in the sample receiving a community service order was reported to be physiologically addicted to drugs, and none was described as an alcoholic, there were many heavy drinkers and users of 'soft' drugs. Previous unreliability in reporting, too, was not necessarily regarded as a good predictor of the offender's likely performance on a community service order; many social enquiry reports recommending such an order mentioned a poor response to supervision in the past.

A decision that an offender was unsuitable for a community service order did not usually stem from a fear that the individual would commit another offence while on a work placement: that was a rare occurrence. It was rather a result of an assessment of his likely unreliability or lack of co-operation, or his lack of acceptability to organizations with which he might be placed. In magistrates' courts, therefore, the actual nature of the offence was only a minor consideration; for example, offenders convicted of violence were as likely to be given a community service order as imprisonment.

Nevertheless, these personal characteristics had to be taken into consideration in assessing suitability, and inevitably they had the effect of narrowing down the field of the more serious offenders who could be considered for the sentence. That, of course, did not *necessarily* lead to its use for the less serious offender, but it placed an additional pressure upon courts in that direction.

Women offenders posed another problem. Since they were apparently subject to more lenient treatment than men, they did not usually attract imprisonment until a later point in their criminal careers. Hence they were more likely to be unstable or otherwise personally unsuitable. As a consequence, the use of the community service order as an alternative to custody for women was usually precluded by personal characteristics. The Nottingham organizer specified two particular areas of difficulty:

> First, whether or not instability of personality and behaviour is a more general feature among women offenders, it certainly appears to be more common among those suggested for Community Service consideration. This may be due to the fact that the more stable women are effectively dealt with by other methods such as probation, leaving a minority who are not influenced and eventually become candidates for Community Service Orders. Secondly, it seems probable from experience of those actually made the subject of Orders that women offenders are more vulnerable to stress and change in their domestic environment, and that the pattern of their environment may change more dramatically and unexpectedly during the term of an Order, than appears to be likely with male offenders. For example, financial pressure may suddenly produce a need to take up employment, pregnancy may occur, children may develop health and behaviour problems, husbands may have accidents or change their employment to a type which imposes new restrictions on their wives' availability. In effect, the suitability of women offenders tends to involve the suitability—and particularly the stability—of their entire family, and this is obviously far more difficult to predict. (Nottinghamshire Probation and After-care Service, 1975: p. 10)

Finally, personal characteristics sometimes limited the number of hours that an offender could reasonably be expected to perform. For example, shift work or extensive overtime, responsibility for looking after children, poor physical health, or limited motivation, could all reduce the offender's availability for work and restrict the court's choice of an appropriate number of hours on a tariff basis. Thus probation officers, especially in Nottingham, were encouraged to comment on the length of order that the offender would be most likely to manage successfully, and to pay specific attention to characteristics which might limit his availability or motivation for work. This was analogous to comments about an offender's means to pay a fine or to manage a particular rate of fine repayment. It was a further encroachment upon the strict application of tariff principles.

The over-all effect, therefore, of the policy underlying the community service order and the way in which it is implemented in practice, is ambivalence and confusion over the type of offender for whom it should properly be used. This, in turn, has had the inevitable consequence of reducing its scope to act as an alternative to custody and lowering its over-all tariff position.

Conclusion

This book has described the development and use of the community service order in five probation and after-care areas in England, with particular reference to the sentencing practice of six selected magistrates' courts. It has been shown that there were significant variations between courts in the frequency with which the community service order was used, and that a low use of it was associated with a low use of other non-custodial measures and a high use of custodial sentences. Most of the apparent disparities between courts in sentencing practice could not be explained, from a tariff perspective, by local differences in offence and offender characteristics.

When, however, the offenders receiving a community service order were not taken as a whole, this neat picture altered. The overall tariff position of the community service order was affected by considerable internal disparity, so that in each court the sentence was imposed upon offenders who had committed crimes of widely differing degrees of seriousness. While some were similar to those sentenced to imprisonment, others were at a stage where such a sentence would have been highly unlikely. It has been suggested that this in turn was partly because the philosophy and practice of the community service order was riddled with confusion and ambiguity, so that there was no consensus, either within or between areas and courts, on the types of offenders for whom the sentence was appropriate, the reasons for which it should be imposed, or the way in which it should be administered. Thus its initial purpose of effecting a substantial reduction in the prison population was blurred.

The community service order is evidently no nearer to achieving coherence and consistency, in its application as a tariff sentence and in its penal objectives, than it was when it was first introduced. For example, Pease and West have advocated that 'clear and explicit commitment to the use of community service as a tariff sentence (in lieu of a custodial sentence) should be encouraged'

(Pease and West, 1977: p. 18), while the Advisory Council on the Penal System (Home Office, 1977) and Wootton (1977) have repeatedly urged its extension to non-imprisonable offences. There is not even clear agreement that the issue needs resolving. The former community service organizer in Inner London observed during the experimental period:

> Before community service orders are extended there should be an examination of the philosophies involved, in order that we all march on in step to the next stage. The experience thus far has shown that there is little harmony between the sentencers and those who have to implement community service orders. It seems essential to resolve these issues if the future of community service is to be of use to courts and satisfying to the probation service. (Knapman, 1974: p. 162)

In stark contrast, in the same year the Durham community service organizer declared with supreme optimism:

> With dedication, tolerance, commitment and a professional act of faith the Probation and After-care Service can reconcile all these competing objectives [punishment, treatment, deterrence, rehabilitation, group therapy, atonement, reparation], using the statutory authority of the order to control and care for the offender. The overriding aims are the prevention of crime, the welfare of the offender, and the protection and wellbeing of the community. These are not only compatible but synonymous. (Durham Probation and After-care Service, 1974: p. 7)

Such diversity of opinion on the nature of the community service order and the way in which it should develop has been its hallmark since it was first mooted.

In this respect, a possible parallel can be drawn with the development and use of imprisonment as a penal sanction. For many decades custodial sanctions were believed to fulfil many positive, but apparently contradictory, societal functions: they could punish, deter, reform, and isolate. This belief has now been supplanted by a blind faith in community-based measures, a faith which has been given added force by their economic advantages. The community service order is one such example. The initial muted wait-and-see attitude which accompanied the setting up of the experimental schemes has been replaced by a widespread belief in the ability of the sentence to serve a whole variety of penal functions. Thus there are increasing signs that it is coming to be used indiscriminately as the new panacea in penal treatment. And as with imprisonment, it is inevitable that the attempt to make a single sentence serve a whole host of purposes will result in failure; we are simply transferring 'our inflated expectations from one structure to another' (Anttila, 1975: p. 80).

The effects of such diversity of opinion on the use of the sentence by the courts cannot be ignored. The sentencing practice of the courts studied here indicates that, if disparities and inconsistencies in the application and implementation of the community service order are to be reduced, the tariff location of the sentence must be clarified and its objectives set in order of priority. And there are several cogent reasons why inconsistencies should be minimized as far as possible.

First, when potentially incompatible objectives are pursued within the same sentence and inconsistencies in practice emerge as a result, then conflict inevitably emerges between one objective and another in the resolution of particular issues. As that continues to happen, discontent among those who believe that success in accomplishing one objective is being neutralized by the need to cater for another will probably increase, and the eventual consequence will be disillusion by sentencers, probation officers, and the community alike.

It is true, of course, that it is notoriously difficult to find any agreement on issues of penal policy, and many worthwhile reforms and innovations would have been stifled by any requirement that consensus be reached on their objectives. Nevertheless, the resulting pragmatism may, in the final analysis, produce effects which are distinctly counter-productive. If, for example, the community service order is used often as an alternative penalty to a fine, or as a rehabilitative measure in lieu of a probation order, but at the same time a custodial sentence is regularly being imposed for breach, the result could easily be an increase rather than a reduction in the population of penal establishments. There is, indeed, some suspicion that that is precisely what occurred following the introduction of the suspended sentence in 1967 (Sparks, 1971; Radzinowicz, 1971). Ambivalent policies can produce consequences which satisfy no one.

Secondly, inconsistent policies and practices do not allow for a consistent criterion by which the success of the community service order can be assessed. As the fourth annual report on the Inner London scheme stated:

> If one yardstick of success is to be the percentage of orders successfully completed, then the results are encouraging as the statistical analysis shows. Success in other terms may depend for its criteria on where one stands, on attitudes towards the treatment/punishment debate and how the effects of community service are perceived. (Inner London Probation and After-care Service, 1976: p. 1)

If the community service order is intended to be primarily

rehabilitative, at least in the sense of the prevention of further offending, then reconviction rates (in comparison with other available penal measures) provide the obvious criterion of success. If it is to be primarily a punishment or a means of benefiting the community, then the normal completion of orders, under a consistent and equitable system of control, might be a better criterion of success. At present people seem content to ask whether it works (for example, Harding, 1973: p. 17; Griffiths, 1977: p. 193). But as the sentence may work from one standpoint and at the same time be a failure from another, this simply evades the issue. Proceedings for breach of a community service order, for instance, might well be seen as evidence of its failure as a rehabilitative measure; however, in terms of punishment they might be seen as evidence of its consistent and successful implementation.

This does not mean, of course, that a single basic penal aim should be pursued to the exclusion of all others. That would be neither possible nor desirable. But what needs to be recognized is that within a single sentence, different objectives may *sometimes* be contradictory rather than complementary. A complete reconciliation of such objectives can therefore be achieved only by specifying which aim should predominate in a situation of conflict. The issue is not the *exclusion* of aims, but the *primacy* of aims.

Which of the various philosophies and objectives of the community service order, then, should be given primary emphasis? On the one hand, there is little evidence that it is likely to be markedly more effective as a rehabilitative measure than other sentences. On the other hand, it does impose a real, and sometimes extensive, obligation upon the offender, while usually reaping considerable benefits for the community as well. Therefore, in addition to being a harsh enough penalty to serve as a viable alternative to custody, it also has an appeal as an alternative to custody in cost–benefit terms.

It is true that its economic benefits should not be overestimated, at least in the short term. Until such time as it effects a large enough reduction in the prison population to enable the closure of an institution or to prevent the building of a new one, its financial advantages in the short term are only marginal. For example, during the first year of the scheme in Ipswich, the cost amounted to £14,500, not including rent, lighting or heating for the premises occupied by the community service staff. In the same period a total of about 3,500 hours were worked. Assuming an average length of 120 hours for an order, that represents 29.2 completed orders, or a minimum cost per order of nearly £500. In comparison, on 13 October 1975 the weekly cost of keeping a man in prison was estimated at about £62 (H.C. Debates, 897: col. 580). Once the schemes are established and the number of orders increase, the cost is considerably reduced. At the beginning of 1977, the direct cost (in terms of staffing, supervision, equipment, etc.) of an order in Nottingham was estimated at £250. Nevertheless, in areas without large urban populations the current caseload remained small even after two years of operation, and the cost therefore remained quite high. Thus the community service order is certainly more expensive than most other non-custodial options, especially the fine, and will prove its direct benefits in economic terms only if it enables a substantial reduction, or prevents a substantial increase, in the population of penal institutions.

However, when the value of the work which is performed is also taken into account, then its advantages over a custodial sentence become much more pronounced, both in economic and humane terms. For that reason, I suggest that it should be clearly established as an alternative to custody. In that case, however, it should not at the same time be established primarily as a rehabilitative measure, because that would probably result in the gradual erosion of its tariff position. Under a firmly entrenched tariff sentencing structure, courts will not regard a measure as equally appropriate for offenders of widely differing degrees of gravity. As a consequence, until such time (if ever) as the community service order were shown to be markedly effective in reducing recidivism rates, as a rehabilitative measure it would come to be used in a parallel fashion to the probation order: sometimes for the serious offender who was thought particularly likely to respond to it, but more often for the minor offender for whom a severe penalty was not required on a tariff basis. It is a mistake to believe that a penal measure can often serve as an alternative to custody if its penal content is relegated to the background, or if it is also used for a whole range of less serious offenders.

Of course, any policy which effectively restricted the use of the community service order to circumstances which justified a custodial sentence would probably decrease the number of orders made. Whatever the pressure to use custodial sentences as a last resort, they will still retain an appeal, at least for the foreseeable future, as a preventive measure. There may thus be inherent limitations upon the extent to which a new non-custodial measure can divert offenders from a sentence of immediate custody, since it will still be applied largely to those who are 'safe', that is, those either who are thought very unlikely to reoffend or whose reoffending would be tolerable. For that reason Lord Morris suggested in Parliament in 1972 that the requirement that sentencers did not send people to prison unless no other method was appropriate was merely setting out in statutory form 'what has been the recognized principle of every judge and every magistrate. . . . Judges struggle to avoid sending people to prison' (H.L. Debates 332: col. 660). To the extent that this is true, the hope that the community service order would divert a substantial number of offenders from custodial sentences may have been unduly optimistic. Indeed, it is not without significance that of the courts studied here, with the exception of Medway, those with a more severe sentencing practice made less frequent use of the community service order, in proportion to the other sentences selected for comparison. It might have been hoped that, in the courts which made greater use of imprisonment, there would have been more scope for the use of the community service order as an alternative to it; in fact, in general the reverse was true.

By the same token, practical features of a sentence that is being implemented in the community (as described in Chapter 8) further restrict its use for serious offenders to those who are not thought to pose an unacceptable risk and who would not therefore place the scheme, and the maintenance of community goodwill, in jeopardy. For the rest, at least without a change in public and judicial attitudes, a custodial sentence remains both the last resort and the only suitable measure.

Nevertheless, there is still a widespread belief that there is scope for a reduction in the use of imprisonment, and the philosophical appeal of the community service order makes it an ideal candidate to effect such a reduction. If it is to utilize its full potential in that regard, however, then its tariff position must be clearly established.

But how can sentencing practice be controlled to ensure that the sentence is used as an alternative to custody? An official pronouncement on the objectives of the sentence, and the types of offenders for whom it should be used, would not necessarily resolve the present conflict and ambiguity. The task of influencing sentencing policy and practice is very difficult in a system which relies upon the treasured independence of the judiciary from executive interference, and which typically confers wide discretionary powers in the performance of judicial functions. It must be admitted that, within the legislatively prescribed maximum penalties for particular offences, statutory attempts to control the exercise of judicial discretion in sentencing do not seem to have had conspicuous success (Thomas, 1974; Ashworth, 1977).

Thomas distinguishes three different statutory techniques that have been employed. The first he describes as a 'bold exhortation— the use of a statutory formula indicating a legislative preference for a particular policy, but not including any effective mandatory element' (Thomas, 1974: p. 143). Provisions restricting the use of imprisonment for first offenders, young adult offenders, and more recently those without a previous sentence of imprisonment, to those for whom the court deems no other method appropriate (ss. 19–20 Powers of Criminal Courts Act 1973) illustrate this approach. The second technique is the restriction of a sentence by criteria other than legal categories of offence. An example is the provision which was inserted in the Criminal Justice Act 1972 to the effect that the court should not impose a suspended sentence unless the case appears to be one in which a sentence of imprisonment would have been appropriate in the absence of a power to suspend. The third technique is the requirement that the court impose a particular measure (such as disqualification from driving) unless special circumstances render it inappropriate or unjust.

All three of these methods of controlling discretion have had only limited impact on sentencing practice. The apparent failure of the third method, for example, is illustrated by the reluctance of three of the courts in this study to activate suspended sentences upon breach. Specific guidance could, of course, be given via a practice direction from the Lord Chief Justice[1] or, in the case of magistrates' courts, via a Home Office circular, but these too could be easily subverted unless an effective machinery existed to check the decisions made. Without a regular review by an appellate body, it may be that attempts to structure the exercise of discretion within the bounds of the statutory maxima may be effective only to the extent that they accord with the existing sentiments of sentencers.

The prescription of penal objectives raises the parallel problem of inter-organizational tension and conflict. No systematic evidence has been adduced in this book to show the reasons for magistrates' choice of sentence, or the extent to which this concurred with probation officers' views on the purposes of the community service order. However, the existence of competing values and ideologies between different agencies in the criminal justice system has been documented elsewhere (for example, Wheeler, 1968: chs 3 and 4; Giller and Morris, 1976; Bottomley, 1977). Moreover, there is at present no centralized machinery by which disputes or conflicting values within the legal bands can be managed or resolved. The community service order, therefore, is a clear example of the confusion which permeates the whole system. So long as separate and independent agencies exist, with different perspectives on their roles in imposing or implementing a sentence, the official formulation of specific objectives may have little effect: in meeting the values of one agency, they will conflict with the values of another agency and are therefore likely to be resisted or subverted.

Despite this, a clarification of the objectives and of the tariff location of the community service order is a necessary, although perhaps not a sufficient, condition for any substantial reduction in inconsistencies in the application and implementation of the sentence. And unless such a clarification is attempted, there is a distinct possibility that the present enthusiasm for the sentence will give way to pessimism and disillusion. Moreover, there is greater opportunity to offer principles to govern the use of a new sentence than of one which is already firmly established: once roles and objectives are entrenched, the formulation of a consistent policy from above will not easily shift them. This opportunity has been largely neglected in the case of the community service order; and the blame for that must rest, partly with the Wootton Committee, which introduced and fostered the ambiguity, and partly with the Home Office, which has made little attempt to resolve it.

Appendix

The statistical analysis of the characteristics of the offenders in each court was carried out on a computer by the use of a statistical package program for the social sciences (Nie *et al.*, 1975). The data presented in this book were mainly produced from cross-tabulation analysis, which made possible an examination of the percentages in each discrete category of each variable.

The significance of differences between courts and between sentences was measured in all cases by the *chi-square* test (denoted by χ^2). The conventional level of significance ($p < .05$) was adopted; but this, of course, is an arbitrary dividing line and comment on other differences was not excluded merely because they did not reach this level. The χ^2 test is a valid test of significance only when the expected frequencies are at least five in 80 per cent or more of the cells in the table. Thus in some instances in the foregoing analysis the statistical significance of differences could not be tested, so that more reliance had to be placed upon numbers and percentages, without corresponding statistical inferences, than was strictly desirable.

Although the small number of community service orders in some courts was a problem, it should be remembered that they included all orders made in those courts during the first year of the operation of the scheme, and therefore furnished more information about the use of the sentence than would have been the case if a mere random sample of offenders receiving a community service order had been studied. In other words, although the numbers, for example in Bedford, were too small to allow them to be used with confidence as a measure of the tariff in that court, they nevertheless accurately described the use of the community service order in Bedford during the first year.

The level of significance of a difference, as indicated by χ^2, does not of course indicate the size of that difference. The use of χ^2 by itself could thus be misleading since, for a given strength of association between two variables, it increases linearly with the size of the sample. A statistically significant relationship could therefore be obtained with a small difference and a large sample, although the result might have little practical significance. Conversely, a relationship might not be significant in a small sample, even if the difference was large.

In analysing the courts' sentencing practice, therefore, two statistical measures of association were used to indicate the strength and direction of the differences. First, in comparing the characteristics of offenders given all sentences in each court (Chapter 6), the statistic *gamma* (denoted by γ) was used for all variables measured on an ordinal level. The γ test is suitable where the independent variable is a discontinuous variable with a small number of categories (between three and eight) which are in a definite order. It was chosen in preference to alternative ordinal measures of association, such as the Kendall rank correlation coefficient *tau*, because of its applicability to grouped data such as those collected here. The computational formula of *tau* incorporates corrections for ties, and is therefore more applicable to data in which there are a large number of ranks. When *tau* is used for data grouped into a small number of ranks, the number of ties which occurs depresses the correlation coefficient and tends to disguise the real strength of association. For that reason γ was preferred.

γ takes a value of 0 when there is no relationship between the variables, and a value of ± 1 when there is a perfect relationship. It is, however, difficult to offer an objective criterion by which any particular value of γ can be interpreted. Goodman and Kruskal (1963) devised a conservative test of significance for γ, but the significance of a value on this test still varies according to the numbers involved. It can be stated, however, that any γ coefficient of .19 or more for the data analysed here was significant on χ^2; in addition, smaller values often reached significance.

Secondly, the *phi* correlation (denoted by ϕ) was used as an index of the strength of the differences between sentences (Chapter 7). ϕ is derived from χ^2. It is appropriate for 2×2 tables and is exactly equivalent to Pearson's Product Moment correlation. Like γ, it has a value of 0 in the case of no difference and a value of 1 in the case of a maximum difference (although the maximum value of ϕ is not always as high as 1).

The use of ϕ required that the values of each variable be converted into a dichotomy. This naturally involved the loss of much useful information by divorcing the quantitative analysis from the raw data on which it was based. However, this was probably not a serious handicap. Simon has suggested for example, that dichotomizing will usually have little effect on the predictive power of an independent variable (Simon, 1971: p. 156). In any case, the use of ϕ to indicate the strength of differences was supplemented by reference to the original cross-tabulation analysis in order to reveal any differences which the dichotomies masked.

As in the case of γ, there is no objective criterion by which a particular value of ϕ can be interpreted. Although it is derived from χ^2, the significance on χ^2 of a particular value of ϕ varies according to sample size. The numbers in the analysis varied a great deal, depending on the numbers given in each sentence in each court. In all courts, ϕ coefficients of .30 or more were invariably significant at $p < .05$. However, while in the comparison of sentences in Nottingham coefficients of .12 or over were nearly always significant, in Bedford coefficients over .25 often did not reach significance. Because of this variability depending on the sample size, ϕ values of .12 or over were always regarded as indicating the existence of a difference, whatever the level of significance.

The use of ϕ also enabled the effect of other variables to be taken into account by the calculation of the partial ϕ correlation,[1] so that it could be seen whether differences between sentences in respect of one variable could be explained by reference to some other variable. The use of partial ϕ was preferable to any form of partial correlation analysis where the control is statistical rather than literal. Although such analysis would have enabled the influence of several control variables to be assessed simultaneously, it would not have exposed interactive effects and thus would have been difficult to interpret.

These statistical techniques were simple and obviously did not give a perfect description of the relationship between variables. However, they were thought preferable to more sophisticated multivariate techniques for two reasons.

First, techniques such as multiple regression analysis or discriminant analysis, both of which allow the step-wise selection of the combination of variables which best discriminate between two groups, typically necessitate assumptions of linearity and additivity. Although linearity is by definition a feature of dichotomous variables, there was no reason to believe that their effect here was additive; it was quite possible that some would interact in non-additive ways.

Secondly, in every court the number of cases receiving each sentence was far too small to justify the use of multiple regression methods (Simon, 1971: p. 154; West and Farrington, 1973: p. 150). The attachment of weights to individual variables, and the combination of variables to provide the 'best fit' on the regression line, inevitably entails the possibility of capitalization on chance variations. Ideally, too, the discriminating power of the optimal combination should be tested on a validation sample. That was not possible in this case, and it was likely that the discrimination obtained would have been highly unstable and subject to large shrinkage. Simon (1971) found that even a sample size of 270 was far too small. As West and Farrington have stated, the use of very refined statistical techniques to analyse rough data of the type collected here 'has always seemed to us like taking a sledge-hammer to crack a nut' (West and Farrington, 1977: p. 148). The small numbers in each group also prevented the use of hierarchical splitting techniques such as Predictive Attribute Analysis or Association Analysis (Wilkins and MacNaughton-Smith, 1964; MacNaughton-Smith, 1965), which allows for non-linear and non-additive interactions.

Despite the simplicity of the statistical methods employed here, therefore, they are likely to provide at least as accurate a picture as multivariate techniques would have done, perhaps even more so. Moreover, they have the advantage of easy presentation and ready interpretation.

Notes

Introduction

1. Their research has been published in two separate reports: Pease *et al.* (1975), and Pease *et al.* (1977).

Part one—legislation and practice

1 The background

1. For examples of studies of the development and extension of probation for offenders in the last half of the nineteenth century and the twentieth see Bochel (1976) and King (1969). There is no doubt that the official scheme of probation supervision introduced in 1907 was designed in part to keep some offenders out of institutions: it was confidently asserted in the Parliamentary debates on the Probation of Offenders Act that it would 'to a large extent empty our jails' (Parliamentary Debates, 179: col. 1487).

2. A more thorough discussion of these themes can be found in Hawkins (1975) and Scull (1977).

3. See the later summaries of research by Martinson (1974); Lipton *et al.* (1975); and Brody (1976).

4. There is no evidence that this rise was caused by higher courts dealing with a smaller proportion of all indictable offences. In fact, just the opposite; the proportion of all indictable offences dealt with by higher courts actually fell during the same period.

5. Attendance centres, established by the Criminal Justice Act 1948, had until then been restricted to those aged 12–16 (see McClintock, 1961). The Advisory Council's proposals resulted in the establishment of two centres for young adults at Manchester and Greenwich in 1958 and 1964 respectively.

6. This finding went largely unchallenged in the 1960s, although it has been subject to recent criticism (Bottoms, 1973).

7. This development in the United Kingdom and elsewhere in the years immediately preceding 1960, has been analysed by Schafer (1970).

8. Such a scheme was established on a non-statutory basis in 1964 following the report of a Home Office Working Party (Home Office, 1961).

9. For example, Hauser (1963); del Vecchio (1969); and Gibbens (1970).
10. For a description of the operation of this scheme, see Wilce (1973) and Kelmanson (1976).
11. For the text of this speech, see *The Magistrate*, 1976, vol. 32, no. 12, p. 188.
12. For a description of periodic detention work centres, see New Zealand Justice Department, 1973.

2   The legislation

1. s.49 of the 1972 Act, which authorized the imposition of a community service order in lieu of imprisonment for fine default, was not consolidated in the 1973 Act, but neither was it repealed. The section has not yet been implemented.
2. I have discussed this issue and other difficulties inherent in the legislation elsewhere (Young, 1977).
3. For a fuller discussion of this issue, see Ford (1972) and Bean (1976).
4. See, for example, Hardiker (1977). She found that probation officers rarely thought exclusively of the offender's needs or the possibilities of treatment without consideration of the offence or the policy of the court. Thus she described a recommendation for sentence as 'the organizational procedure which enables a probation officer to negotiate his treatment preferences mediated by various offence, offender and social control factors'.
5. I am grateful to Mr David Thomas for allowing me access to this unreported case.
6. For example, in studies by McWilliams (1968); Ford (1972); and Perry (1974).
7. A useful summary of these studies can be found in White (1972).

3   The philosophy

1. This debate is discussed more fully in the next chapter.
2. The research was undertaken during 1976 and 1977.
3. The selection of this sample, and the more detailed study of the sentencing practice of the courts, is described in Part II.
4. Hereafter the courts and usually the probation areas are referred to as Ipswich, Peterborough, Medway, Nottingham, Bedford, and Cambridge.
5. See Moberly, 1968: pp. 186–200; Honderich, 1969: pp. 34–40; Doyle, 1967.
6. This, though, has been modified in some cases in recent years by the greater use of short periods of supervision with specific objectives agreed with the client in advance. For this type of approach, see, for example, Reid and Epstein (1972).
7. This study has serious methodological limitations. Not only was it restricted to those who had successfully completed orders, but it had less than 50 per cent co-operation rate: only 100 out of 207 offenders who had completed orders could be interviewed. Despite these limitations and the

difficulties of generalizing from them, the offenders' comments are of interest.

8. See, for example, the criteria suggested by the Kent community service organizer during the two-year experimental period (Sussex, 1974: p. 14).

9. Statutes of the Realm 1 Edward VI, c.3, cited by Nicholls, 1967: pp. 129–30. This Act provided that able-bodied vagrants who would not work could be seized by their former masters and made slaves for two years. If no master could be found, they could be enslaved by the borough and employed on road-building and other public work.

10. See Inner London Probation and After-care Service, 1976: pp. 61–4. Bulldog Manpower Services Ltd is a firm offering full-time salaried employment to young male offenders with poor work histories. It is broadly modelled upon the structure of the Wildcat Service Corporation in New York (see Vera Institute of Justice, 1975).

4 Administration and Practice

1. Social enquiry reports that included a positive recommendation for a community service order were presumed to have been instigated by the probation officer unless there was evidence to the contrary. Therefore these figures may not be entirely accurate. Nevertheless, it is probable that either the court register, the social enquiry report, or the community service file would have recorded nearly all the cases initiated by the court.

2. See, for example, the reactions of probation officers to the Younger Report proposals in *Probation Journal*, 1974, vol. 21, no. 4.

3. For a full discussion of the nature of a 'tariff' system of sentencing, see *supra*, pp. 76–81.

4. In almost all cases, non-co-operation and eventual failure on a community service order takes the form of absenteeism rather than bad work or misbehaviour on the work site.

Part two—the use of the community service order by the courts

5 The method of research

1. The study formed the major part of an unpublished Ph.D. dissertation presented to the University of Cambridge (Young, 1978).

2. For the most part the analysis was done on a computer using a statistical package program for the social sciences (Nie *et al.*, 1975).

3. For thorough reviews of these studies, see Hood and Sparks (1970: ch. 5) and Bottomley (1973: ch. 4).

4. The other recognized departure from tariff principles is in the opposite direction: the extended sentence and the life sentence may be imposed to protect the public against the 'persistent' and 'dangerous' offender respectively, and may involve detention for longer than the tariff would have justified. This departure, however, is not relevant to magistrates' courts.

6 Variations in the use of the sentence

1. The χ^2 test of significance was used and the conventional level of significance of p < .05 was adopted. It should be noted that there were ten occasions in Nottingham and one in Peterborough when either a suspended sentence or a probation order was imposed in conjunction with a community service order, although of course for a different offence. Only the community service order was counted in such cases; however, this occurred too infrequently to alter significantly the differences in the proportionate use of the suspended sentence or the probation order.

2. The terms 'severe' and 'lenient' are used here to indicate a particular level of intervention, and are not intended as an evaluative comment about the appropriateness of those measures for individual offenders.

3. The statistics used (principally *chi-square* and *gamma*) are described in the Appendix. A fuller discussion of the use of these statistics, and of the nature and interpretation of the differences between courts, can be found in my unpublished Ph.D. dissertation (Young, 1978).

4. At the conventional level of significance (p < .05) there is less than one chance in twenty that a significant result is achieved by chance.

5. s. 19(2) Powers of Criminal Courts Act 1973.

6. The differences, though, were not susceptible to tests of statistical significance, as the expected frequencies in the table were too small. (For a χ^2 test of significance to be applied there must be an expected frequency of less than five in fewer than 20 per cent of the cells.)

7. The pilot areas attracted so much attention and so many resources that the sentence was likely to appeal to sentencers for that reason alone.

7 The location of the community service order in the tariff

1. The data have been set out in more detailed form elsewhere (Young, 1978). This chapter presents the main conclusions that can be drawn from the data.

2. See Pease *et al.*, 1975: p. 29; Inner London Probation and After-care Service, 1975: Appendix 4; Nottinghamshire Probation and After-care Service, 1975: Appendix B; Durham County Probation and After-care Service, 1975: p. 13; Sussex, 1974: Appendix XIII.

3. This did not appear to result from a high proportion of serious offences committed by that age group. Of the eleven young adult offenders given imprisonment, only two were convicted of violence, and one of burglary or forgery.

4. For the purposes of comparison, housewives were classified as employed and having regular work habits.

5. Ipswich ϕ .38, p < .002; Peterborough ϕ .28, p < .06; Medway ϕ .39, p < .0002; Bedford ϕ .25, significance not known; Nottingham ϕ .23, p < .0001; Cambridge ϕ .37, p < .006.

6. In Peterborough ϕ .23, p < .02; in Nottingham ϕ .38, p < .0001.

7. ϕ .29.

8. ϕ .32, p < .005.

9. The most serious current offence was taken to be that for which one of the selected sentences was imposed. On the few occasions when a community service order was combined with a suspended sentence or a probation order, then it was assumed that the most serious current offence was that for which the community service order was imposed. If concurrent sentences, or consecutive sentences of the same length, were given then, in general the statutory maxima were used as a guide to rank offences in order of seriousness.

10. ϕ .20.

11. $p < .0005$.

Conclusion

1. This device has been used in the past to guide courts in the use of particular sentences, for example, preventive detention and corrective training (see [1962] Crim. L.R. 308).

Appendix

1. A weighted partial ϕ, in the case of a dichotomous control variable, was obtained by the formula

$$\frac{\phi_1 N_1 + \phi_2 N_2}{N_1 + N_2}$$

(see Blalock, 1972: p. 310); that is, the ϕ obtained in the table for each value of the control variable was multiplied by the number of cases in that table, the results added, and then divided by the total number of cases over both tables.

References

The page number(s) at the end of an entry refers to the page(s) of this book on which the publication is mentioned.

Abrams, M. (1959), *The Teenage Consumer*, London, Press Exchange. *(p. 16)*

Anttila, I. (1975), 'Probation and Parole: Social Control or Social Service', *International Journal of Criminology and Penology*, 3: pp. 79–84. *(p. 136)*

Ashworth, A.J. (1977), 'Justifying the First Prison Sentence', *Criminal Law Review*, pp. 661–73. *(p. 140)*

Bean, P. (1976), *Rehabilitation and Deviance*, London, Routledge & Kegan Paul. *(p. 148)*

Blalock, H.M. (1972), *Social Statistics*, (2nd ed.), New York, McGraw-Hill. *(p. 151)*

Blom-Cooper, L. (1976) 'The Parameters of Sentencing', *Howard Journal*, 15(2): pp. 6–12. *(p. 78)*

Bochel, D. (1976), *Probation and After-care: its Development in England and Wales*, Edinburgh, Scottish Academic Press. *(p. 147)*

Bottomley, A.K. (1973), *Decisions in the Penal Process*, London, Martin Robertson. *(p. 149)*

—— (1977), 'Conflict and Communication in Criminal Justice', *Howard Journal*, 15(3): pp. 3–11. *(p. 141)*

Bottoms, A.E. (1973), 'The Efficacy of the Fine: the Case for Agnosticism', *Criminal Law Review*, p. 543. *(p. 147)*

Bourke, C. (1976), 'Community Service: a Different View', *Justice of the Peace*, 140(33): pp. 441–3. *(p. 119)*

Brody, S.R. (1976), *The Effectiveness of Sentencing*, Home Office Research Study no. 35, London, H.M.S.O. *(p. 147)*

Committee on Local Authority and Allied Personal Social Services (1968), *Report*, (Chairman: Frederic Seebohm), London, H.M.S.O., Cmd. 3703. *(pp. 15, 16)*

Conservative Party Study Group (1966), *Crime Knows No Boundaries*, (Chairman: Rt Hon. Peter Thorneycroft, M.P.), London, Conservative Political Centre. *(pp. 5, 13, 16)*

Conservative Political Centre (1959), *The Challenge of Leisure*, C.P.C. no. 203, London, Conservative Political Centre. *(p. 16)*

Davies, M. (1974), 'Social Inquiry for the Courts: an Examination of the Current Position in England and Wales', *British Journal of Criminology*, 14(1): pp. 18–33. *(p. 30)*

Del Vecchio, G. (1969), 'The Struggle against Crime', in Acton, H.B. (ed.), *The Philosophy of Punishment*, London, Macmillan & Co. *(p. 148)*

Departmental Committee on Corporal Punishment (1938), *Report*, (Chairman: Sir Edward Cadogan), London, H.M.S.O., Cmd. 5684. *(p. 11)*

Departmental Committee on Persistent Offenders (1932), *Report*, (Chairman: Sir John Dove-Wilson), London, H.M.S.O., Cmd. 4090. *(p. 79)*

Departmental Committee on Prisons (the Gladstone Committee, 1895). *(p. 79)*

Departmental Committee on the Probation Service (1962), *Report*, (Chairman: R.P. Morison), London, H.M.S.O., Cmd. 1650. *(p. 29)*

Doyle, J.F. (1967), 'Justice and Legal Punishment', in Acton, H.B. (ed.) (1969), *The Philosophy of Punishment*, London, Macmillan & Co. *(p. 148)*

Durham County Probation and After-care Service (1974), *Community Service Orders*, Durham, Probation and After-care Service. *(p. 136)*

_____ (1975), *Community Service Orders, an Evaluation Report of Two Years of Community Service by Offenders in Durham County*, Durham, Probation and After-care Service. *(pp. 39, 44, 48, 55, 150)*

_____ (1977), *Community Service Committee: Annual Report Incorporating Progress Report no. 12*, Durham, Probation and After-care Service. *(p. 128)*

Flegg, D. *et al.* (1976), *Community Service Consumer Survey 1973–1976*, Nottingham, Probation and After-care Service. *(p. 41)*

Ford, P. (1972), *Advising Sentencers*, Oxford, Basil Blackwell. *(p. 148)*

Fry, M. (1957), 'Justice for Victims', in *The Observer*, 7/7/57.

Gibbens, T.C. (1970), 'Treatment at Liberty', *Annals of International Criminology*, 9(1): pp. 9–30. *(p. 148)*

Giller, H.J. and Morris, A. (1976), 'Children who Offend: Care, Control or Confusion?', *Criminal Law Review*: pp. 656–65. *(p. 141)*

Ginsberg, M. (1965), *On Justice in Society*, London, Heinemann. *(p. 75)*

Goodman, L.A. and Kruskal, W.A. (1963), 'Measures of Association for Cross Classifications', *American Statistical Association Journal*: pp. 310–64. *(p. 144)*

Greenberg, D.F. (1975), 'Problems in Community Corrections', *Issues of Criminology*, 10(1): pp. 1–33. *(p. 4)*

Griffiths, R. (1977), 'Community Service by Offenders', *New Law Journal*, 126: pp. 169–71 and 193–5. *(p. 69, 138)*

Hardiker, P. (1977), 'Social Work Ideologies in the Probation Service', *British Journal of Social Work*, 7(2): pp. 131–54. *(p. 148)*

Harding, J. (1973), 'Community Service—a Beginning', *Probation Journal*, 19(1): pp. 13–17. *(p. 138)*

_____ (1974), 'The Offender and the Community', *Social Work Today*, 5(16): pp. 478–81. *(p. 48)*

Hauser, R. (1963), 'Prison Reform and Society', *Prison Service Journal*, 3(9): pp. 2–18. *(pp. 18, 148)*

Hawkins, K. (1975), 'Alternatives to Imprisonment', in McConville, S. (ed) (1975), *The Use of Imprisonment: Essays i the Changing State of English Penal Policy*, London, Routledge & Kegan Paul. *(p. 147)*

Home Office: Advisory Council on the Treatment of Offenders (1957), *Alternatives to Short Terms of Imprisonment*, (Chairman: H. Studdy), London, H.M.S.O. *(pp. 4, 8, 11, 12, 21)*

Home Office (1959), *Penal Practice in a Changing Society*, London, H.M.S.O., Cmd. 645. *(p. 12)*

_____: Advisory Council on the Employment of Offenders (1961), *Work of Prisoners*, (Chairman: Sir Wilfred Anson), London, H.M.S.O. *(p. 50)*

_____: Working Party on Compensation for Victims of Crimes of Violence (1961), *Report*, London, H.M.S.O., Cmd. 1406. *(p. 147)*

_____: Advisory Council on the Employment of Offenders (1962), *Work and Vocational Training in Borstals* (England and Wales), (Chairman: Sir Wilfred Anson), London, H.M.S.O. *(p. 50)*

_____: (1964), *The Sentence of the Court,*, London, H.M.S.O., Cmd. 2852. *(p. 10)*

_____: (1965), *The Adult Offender,* London, H.M.S.O., Cmd.2852. *(p.5)*

_____: Working Party on the Place of Voluntary Service in After-care (1967), *Second Report*, (Chairman: The Dowager Marchioness of Reading), London, H.M.S.O. *(p. 14)*

_____ (1969), *People in Prison* (England and Wales), London, H.M.S.O. Cmd.4214. *(p. 7)*

_____: Advisory Council on the Penal System (1970a), *Non-custodial and Semi-custodial Penalties,* (Chairman: Baroness Wootton), London, H.M.S.O. *(pp. ix, 5, 8, 18, 20, 21, 22, 24, 25, 118, 142)*

_____: Advisory Council on the Penal System (1970b), *Reparation by the Offender*, (Chairman: Lord Widgery), London, H.M.S.O. *(p. 13)*

_____: Advisory Council on the Penal System (1970c), *Detention Centres,* (Chairman: Sir Kenneth Younger), London, H.M.S.O. *(pp. 124−5, 149)*

_____: Working Group on Community Service Orders (1971), *Report*, unpublished. *(p. 20)*

_____: (1972), *Criminal Justice Act 1972: A Guide for the Courts*, London, H.M.S.O. *(p. 19)*

_____: Advisory Council on the Penal System (1974), *Young Adult Offenders,* (Chairman: Sir Kenneth Younger), London, H.M.S.O. *(p. 62)*

_____: (1976), *Report on the Work of the Probation and After-care Department 1972−1975*, London, H.M.S.O., Cmd. 6590. *(p. 4)*

_____: Advisory Council on the Penal System (1977), *Powers of the Court Dependent on Imprisonment*, (Chairman: Baroness Serota), London, H.M.S.O. *(p. 136)*

Honderich, T. (1969), *Punishment: the Supposed Justifications*, London, Hutchinson. *(p. 148)*

Hood, R. (1962), *Sentencing in Magistrates' Courts*, London, Stevens & Sons. *(pp. 83, 84)*

_____ (1972), *Sentencing the Motoring Offender*, London, Heinemann. (p. 85)

_____ (1974), 'Criminology and Penal Change', in Hood, R. (ed.), *Crime, Criminology, and Public Policy*, London, Heinemann. *(p. 22)*

Hood, R. and Sparks R.F. (1970), *Key Issues in Criminology*, London, Weidenfeld & Nicolson. *(p. 149)*

Hood R. and Taylor, I. (1968), 'Second Report of the Effectiveness of

Presentence Investigations in Reducing Recidivism', *British Journal of Criminology*, 8(4): pp. 431–4.

Interdepartmental Committee on the Business of the Criminal Courts (1961), *Report*, (Chairman: Mr Justice Streatfeild), London, H.M.S.O., Cmd. 1289. *(pp. 29, 79)*

Inner London Probation and After-care Service (1975), *Community Service by Offenders: a Progress Report of the First Two Years' Operation of the Scheme in Inner London*, London, Probation and After-care Service. *(pp. ix, x, 150)*

—— (1976), *ILPAS '76: a Report of Aspects of the Work . . . to Commemorate the Centenary of Probation in London*, London, Probation and After-care service. *(pp. ix, 49, 137, 149)*

Johnson, A.S. (1976), 'Meditations of a Magistrate', *Justice of the Peace*, 140(43): pp. 580–2. *(p. 119)*

Kelmanson, A. (1976), *The Experience of Giving: Borstal Boys in Full-time Community Service*, London, Community Service Volunteers. *(p. 148)*

King, J.F.S. (ed.) (1969), *The Probation and After-care Service*, (3rd ed.), London, Butterworths. *(p. 147)*

Knapman, E. (1974), 'Community Service Orders—a Rationale', *Justice of the Peace*, 138(12): p. 162. *(p. 136)*

Kneale, W. (1967), 'The Responsibility of Criminals', in Acton, H.B. (ed.) (1969), *The Philosophy of Punishment*, London, Macmillan & Co. *(p. 37)*

Labour Party Study Group (1974), *Crime—a Challenge to Us All*, (Chairman: Lord Longford), London, Transport House. *(pp. 5, 8, 9)*

Lipton, D. *et al.* (1975), *Effectiveness of Correctional Treatment—a Survey of Treatment Evaluation Studies*, Springfield, Praeger. *(p. 147)*

McClintock, F.H. (1961), *Attendance Centres*, London, Macmillan & Co. *(p. 147)*

McNaughton-Smith, P. (1965), 'Some Statistical and other Numerical Techniques for Classifying Individuals', *Studies in the Causes of Delinquency and the Treatment of Offenders, no. 6*, London, H.M.S.O. *(p. 146)*

McWilliams, W., (1968), 'Presentence Study of Offenders: an Interim Report', *Case Conference*, 15(4): pp. 136–9. *(p. 148)*

Martinson, R. (1974), 'What Works: Questions and Answers about Prison Reform', *The Public Interest*, spring issue, p. 23. *(p. 147)*

Ministry of Education: Committee on Youth Service in England and Wales (1960), *Report*, (Chairman: Lady Albemarle), London, H.M.S.O., Cmd. 929. *(p. 16)*

Ministry of Housing and Local Government (1969), *People and Planning: Report of the Committee on Public Participation in Planning*, (Chairman: A.M. Skeffington), London, H.M.S.O. *(p. 14)*

Moberly, W. (1968), *The Ethics of Punishment*, London, Faber & Faber, *(p. 148)*

National Association of Probation Officers (1975), *Report of the Working Party on Community Service Orders*, unpublished. *(p. 128)*

New Zealand Justice Department (1973), *Periodic Detention in New Zealand*, Wellington, Government Printers. *(p. 148)*

Nicholls, G. (1967), *A History of the English Poor Law*, London, Frank Cass & Co. *(p. 149)*

Nie, N.H. *et al.* (1975), *Statistical Package for the Social Sciences*, (2nd ed.), New York, McGraw-Hill. *(pp. 143, 149)*

Nottinghamshire Probation and After-care Service (1975), *Community Service Orders: Report on the Nottinghamshire Experimental Scheme*, Nottingham, Probation and After-care Service. *(pp. 35, 38, 39, 44, 45, 48, 121, 132, 133, 150)*

—— (1976), *Progress Report on the Community Service Order Scheme 1 April 1975–31 March 1976*, Nottingham, Probation and After-care Service.

Oatham, E. and Simon, F.H. (1972), 'Are Suspended Sentences Working?' *New Society*, 21(514): p. 233. *(pp. 86, 87)*

Pease, K. *et al.* (1975), *Community Service Orders*, Home Office Research Study no. 29, London, H.M.S.O. *(pp. x, 32, 55, 73, 122, 126, 147, 150)*

—— (1977), *Community Service Assessed in 1976*, Home Office Research Study no. 39, London, H.M.S.O. *(p. 147)*

Pease, K. and West, J.S.M. (1977), 'Community Service Orders: The Way Ahead', in Crook, A. and Sanderson, N. (eds), *Research Bulletin*, no. 4, London, H.M.S.O. *(pp. 67, 87, 135–6)*

Perry, F.G. (1974), *Information for the Courts: a New Look at Social Inquiry Reports*, Cambridge, Institute of Criminology. *(p. 148)*

Radzinowicz, L. (1966), *Ideology and Crime: a Study of Crime in its Social and Historical Context*, London, Heinemann. *(p. 22)*

—— (1971), 'A Foreseeable Failure', *The Sunday Times*, 24/1/71. *(p. 137)*

Radzinowicz, L. and King, J.F.S. (1977), *The Growth of Crime: the International Experience*, New York, Basic Books. *(p. 35)*

Reid, W.J. and Epstein, L. (1972), *Task-centered Casework*, New York, Columbia University Press. *(p. 148)*

Ringrose, P. *et al.* (1975), *Practical Tasks on Community Service*, unpublished. *(p. 75)*

Royal Commission on the Penal System in England and Wales (1967a), *Written Evidence from Government Departmets, Miscellaneous Bodies, and Individual Witnesses,* London, H.M.S.O. *(pp. 12, 22)*

—— (1967b), *Minutes of Evidence Taken before the Royal Commission,* London, H.M.S.O. *(p. 18)*

Schafer, S. (1970), *Compensation and Restitution to Victims of Crime,* New Jersey, Patterson Smith. *(p. 147)*

Scottish Home and Health Department: Advisory Council on the Treatment of Offenders (1960), *Use of Short Sentences of Imprisonment by the Courts*, (Chairman: H.R. Leslie), Edinburgh, H.M.S.O. *(p. 4)*

Scull, A.T. (1977), *Decarceration*, New Jersey, Prentice-Hall. *(p. 147)*

Seavers, M.J. and Collins, M. (1977), 'Community Service in the Hospital Setting', *Probation Journal*, 24(4): pp. 130–3. *(p. 48)*

Simon, F.H. (1971), *Prediction Methods in Criminology*, Home Office Research Study no. 7, London, H.M.S.O. *(pp. 145, 146)*

Softley, P. (1973), *A Survey of Fine Enforcement*, Home Office Research Study no. 16, London, H.M.S.O. *(p. 10)*

Sparks, R.F. (1965), 'Sentencing by Magistrates: some Facts of Life', in Halmos, P. (ed.), *Sociological Studies in the British Penal Services*, Sociological Review Monograph no. 9, Keele, University of Keele. *(p. 83)*

____ (1971), 'The Use of Suspended Sentences', *Criminal Law Review:* pp. 384–401. *(pp. 86, 87, 137)*

Sussex, J. (1974), *Community Service by Offenders: Year One in Kent,* Chichester, Barry Rose. *(pp. 122, 149, 150)*

Swain, G. (1975), *Community Service Orders: Guidelines for Young Volunteer Organisations*, Leicester, National Youth Bureau. *(p. 44)*

Thomas, D.A. (1974), 'The Control of Discretion in the Administration of Criminal Justice', in Hood, R. (ed.), *Crime, Criminology and Public Policy*, London, Heinemann. *(pp. 140–41)*

____ (1978), *Principles of Sentencing*, (2nd ed), London, Heinemann. *(pp. 77, 78, 80, 119)*

Uglow, S. (1973), *Community Service Orders in Inner London: an Exercise in Illusion*, London, Radical Alternatives to Prison. *(p. 43)*

____ (1975), *Community Service Orders—Some Further Thoughts*, London, Radical Alternatives to Prison. *(p. 43)*

Vera Institute of Justice (1975), *Another Approach to Welfare*, New York, Vera Institute of Justice. *(p. 149)*

Walker, N.D. and Giller, H.J. (eds) (1977), *Penal Policy-making in England*, Cambridge, Institute of Criminology. *(p. 78)*

West, J.S.M. (1976), 'Community Service Orders', in King, J.F.S. and Young, W.S. (eds) (1976), *Control without Custody?*, Cambridge, Institute of Criminology. *(pp. 40, 50, 64, 68, 81)*

____ (1977), 'Community Service Orders—how Different?' *Probation Journal*, 24(4): pp.. 126–30.

West, D.J. and Farrington, D.P. (1973), *Who Becomes Delinquent?* London, Heinemann. *(pp. 145, 146)*

____ (1977), *The Delinquent Way of Life*, London, Heinemann. *(pp. 40, 50)*

Wheeler, S. (ed.) (1968), *Controlling Delinquents*, New York, Wiley. *(pp. 141)*

White, S. (1972), 'The Effect of Social Enquiry Reports on Sentencing Decisions', *British Journal of Criminology*, 12(3): pp. 230–49. *(p. 148)*

Wilce, H. (1973), 'On from Borstal', *New Society*, 23(540); pp. 284–5. *(p. 148)*

Wilkins, L.T. and McNaughton-Smith, P. (1964), 'New Prediction and Classification Methods in Criminology', *Journal of Research in Crime and Delinquency*, 1: pp. 19–32. *(p. 146)*

Winfield, S. (1977), 'What has the Probation Service Done to Community Service', *Probation Journal*, 24(4); pp. 126–30. *(pp. 38, 39)*

Wootton, B. (1959), *Social Science and Social Pathology*, London, George Allen & Unwin. *(p. 10)*

____ (1973), 'Community Service', *Criminal Law Review*, pp. 16–20.

____ (1977), 'Some Reflections on the First Five Years of Community Service', *Probation Journal*, 24(4): pp. 110–12. *(pp. 21, 136)*

Young, W.A. (1977), 'Community Service Orders', *New Law Journal,* 127, pp. 952–5. *(p. 148)*
____ (1978), 'Community Service Orders: The Development of a New Penal Measure', unpublished Ph.D. dissertation presented to the University of Cambridge. *(pp. 149, 150)*

General Index

The letter-by-letter system has been adopted.
Legislation is also grouped under Acts of Parliament.
The cases quoted are referenced under the entry 'case law'.
Reports, studies and committees are detailed in the References section (pp. 152–8), which has become an index by the addition of page references against each.
Complainants and aggrieved persons appear under 'victim', and accused persons under 'offenders'.

sentencing policy *cont.*,
  offences against public decency etc.,
    100–102
  offender's characteristics, local
    differences in, 93–102
  prevalence of offence, factor of,
    113–17
  previous conviction factor, 96–9,
    107–13
  prison, comparative table for courts
    ordering, 89
  probation officers' recommenda-
    tions, 29–32
  Probation Orders, 120–21, 132
    comparative table for courts
      making, 89
  punishment discussed, 35–6
  reasons for reluctance to use new
    measure, 89
  research into disparity in, 74–5
  sex of offender factor, 105
  Social Enquiry Reports, 31
  suspended, 11, 89, 125–7
  variations in, courses open to the
    court as to, 89–102
  where CSO might be unsuitable,
    131–2
  where public order involved, 100–02
  young persons, 3, 31
  see also Acts of Parliament; ambiva-
    lence, policy of; imprisonment;
    legislation; non-custodial;
    offender; philosophy behind
    CSOs; research; tariff structure
sex of offender, 94, 105
Shropshire, pilot scheme for, ix, 35
Silkin, Sam, 23, 36, 43
Social Services Committee, 51
Streatfeild Report, *see under* interdepartmental, 154
study, conclusions of this, 135–42
Suffolk, examination of probation in,
  33–4, 46
  see also Ipswich
supervision, 45–6
suspended sentence, 11, 89, 125–7

tariff structure (sentencing), 76–81
  examples cited, 93, 123–4, 126, 129
  when CSO involved, factors relative,
    103–17
  age, 103–5
  community ties, 106–7
  previous convictions, 107–13
  sex, 105
  see also ambivalence, policy of
Tunbridge Wells, 53

victim of offence, consideration of
  needs of, 13–18
  Voluntary Services Overseas scheme,
    16–17
  volunteers, *see* Community Service
    Volunteers

Waller, Lord Justice, 29–30
Widgery, Lord, 13
Women's Royal Voluntary Service, 61
Wootton Committee, *see* Home Office
  (1970a), 154
Wootton, Lady (Barbara), 5, 25
  see also Home Office (1970a), 154;
    Wootton, 157
work:
  alongside others, 45–6
  assessing suitable, for offender, 54–
  availability of, under CSO, 29–32
  creating desire to, in a new career,
    47–8
  generating desire to, 48–50
  leisure time and, constructive use of,
    46–7
  minimum and maximum hours of,
    under CSOs, ix, 20, 26
  selection of and organising for
    offenders, 57–62
  see also New Careers Movement

Younger, Sir Kenneth, 62
  see also under Home Office, 154
young persons:
  powers of courts to deal with, 3
  Social Enquiry Reports, 31